MOROCCAN ARABIC

Shnoo the Hell is Going On H'naa?

A Practical Guide to Learning Moroccan Darija the Arabic Dialect of Morocco

Welcome to the new and improved 2nd edition – it incorporates reader suggestions and features more details on the transliteration system, additional words, new word lists, and the text has been completely revised and re-edited.

Praise for *Moroccan Arabic* from students, scholars and travelers on both side of the Atlantic:

"Fills a gaping hole in Moroccan Arabic instruction. Based on the first-hand immersion experiences of a native English-speaker who navigated Moroccan culture and language for a year... and as a researcher in Morocco myself, I found it handy."

Nabil Khan, Fulbright Student Grantee

"I love the sense of humor woven throughout - it's an enjoyable read. A great example of collaboration."

Edwin Bodensiek, Dir. of Outreach and Public Relation, CIES - Fulbright, Washington, DC

"A great resource. I wish had this book when I was traveling and researching in Morocco."

Dr Jennifer A Roberson, Professor of Islamic Art, Sonoma State University, California

"Written by a born teacher. This book enhances effective language instruction and builds a collection of everyday conversation resources for Anglo-American students and scholars."

Dr Khalid Amine, Université Abdelmalek Essaadi and President, ICPS – Tangier

"Far from being an ordinary dry text-book, *Shnoo the Hell is Going on H'naa* playfully combines the features of professional linguistics with lively real world sensibilities... [it's] a faithful companion on your travels to the other side of the Atlantic."

Rajae Khaloufi, Arabic Teacher, Translator

"*Shnoo the hell...* hilarious subtitle! Buy it - a great resource for anyone serious about exploring modern Morocco and learning Arabic."

Soufiane Chami, Arabic Teacher, Berkeley, California

Many people contributed to making this book a reality – and by agreement of all, the proceeds from the sale of this book go to support the publishing program at the International Centre for Performance Studies (ICPS) - Tangier, Morocco.

Get involved on Facebook: Collaborative Media International

MOROCCAN ARABIC

Shnoo the Hell is Going On H'naa?

A Practical Guide to Learning Moroccan Darija
the Arabic Dialect of Morocco

—Educational Resources Series—
North Africa

Aaron Sakulich

Rajae Khaloufi, Editor

Produced in partnership by

Collaborative Media International

International Centre for Performance Studies

Denver, Amherst, Tangier

International Centre for Performance Studies (ICPS)
http://www.icpsmorocco.org/

Khalid Amine, PhD
President

Collaborative Media International (CMI)
http://collaborativemedia.blogspot.com/2009/03/darija-text.html

George F Roberson, PhD
Director and Publisher

Thank you for buying this book. By special agreement of all our partners, the proceeds from the sale of this book go to support the ICPS publishing program. This book is sold on Amazon.com and by other fine retailers.

Please join our all-volunteer efforts: suggestions and offers of assistance and collaboration may be contributed by email to: collaborative.media@ymail.com

More information, additional acknowledgements and updates are posted on the webpages listed above.

ISBN 978-0-9824409-3-3

Library of Congress Control Number: 2011920240
Library of Congress subject heading:
Arabic language – Dialects – Morocco
Arabic language – Morocco – Spoken Arabic
Arabic language – Morocco – Conversation and phrasebooks – English

Contents

Introduction to the 2nd Edition

I went to Morocco in September 2007 on a Fulbright grant. I spent my first three months in Fes taking classes in Moroccan Arabic (a.k.a. darija, which means 'dialect'). During this time, I didn't really like any of the textbooks I could find. First, we used a transliterated text with no Arabic script, and then we used a book that had *only* Arabic script. Along the way I got various textbooks from other schools but they still weren't really what I needed. They all seemed like giant tourist phrasebooks, semi-useful, but full of cutesy-poo filler.

What I wanted was the equivalent of a VCR repair manual: just a bare-bones explanation in precise, technical terms of how to do things. I wanted a reference book with simple examples and no fluff. So after a while I decided I'd write a book for myself. I put together all the notes I'd taken in classes, double-checked things with my friends, and this is the final product.

Moroccan Arabic is a very, very variable language. The pronunciation of many words differs somewhat from city to city and region to region. Some of the words I used every day in Fes got me nowhere in Casablanca, and our editor (from Tangier) swears she's never even heard some of the words my friend from Rabat spelled out for me. Although some words vary from place to place, the grammar is constant. After the 1st edition of this book came out, several people complained that I didn't do enough to represent these variations.

To be blunt, trying to do that would be crazy.

Rather than try to address thousands of variations in accents and exact vocabulary, this book is put together to provide a foundation for starting out in Morocco. As you get settled in to your region, you can elaborate and tailor things to suit your situation. If you use a word from this book, and people don't understand, try another one. I make no pretenses that the book is *all* comprehensive, but it's the book I'd have wanted to learn from when I was getting started.

And sure, you could come to Morocco and get along all right in French, Spanish or English, but if you put some effort into learning and using Moroccan Arabic, your time in the land of couscous will be inestimably sweeter. Trust me. I went through learning the language and living there just like you are now.

Despite the valiant efforts of editors on three continents, there are probably some mistakes to be found here. If you find something, or have a suggestion, send us an email! A third edition will reflect your volunteerism and collaboration.

The second edition is a bigger, better version of the first edition, but with the same general structure. Grammatical changes suggested by Abdennebi Elhaloui at ALIF in Fes were incorporated; some additional vocabulary was added; the text was edited to make it easier to read; the layout was fiddled with, hopefully making it a little nicer; and some explanations were put into footnotes, just to try and make the body seem a little cleaner. Also, some jokes were added and some were removed, mostly in new examples.

I hope this helps you!

Aaron Sakulich, PhD
Ann Arbor, Michigan

The Transliteration System

One of the problems I had with the textbooks I've seen is the transliteration. Some were only in English, or Arabic, or transcribed. Some insisted that every letter in Arabic be represented by just one letter in English, while most used the formal alphabet used by academic linguists. For instance, in Arabic, the name 'Morocco' is written المغرب . Here are some examples from various books to represent the same thing:

Mr'Hbaa Bikum!, vol. 1 and 2	lm'ghrib
Moroccan Arabic (Peace Corps)	l-mġrib
From Eastern to Western Arabic	lmɣrb
An introduction to Moroccan Arabic	lmaɣrib
A Short Grammar of Moroccan Arabic	lġerḅ

I don't know what sound a g-with-a-dot-on-it makes, much less a gamma. So each word in this book is written simply the way it sounds to me. Morocco sounds like *Maghreb* and that's why it's written that way. This system is admittedly far from perfect: it's not even always consistent, since two words with the same letters in Arabic sometimes sound different, and are therefore spelled different in this book. Let me repeat, words are presented here the way it sounds to me. For example, I was once roundly chastised for spelling بغيت "bghreet" because the word doesn't contain the Arabic 'r' (ر). But that's the way it sounds, so that's the way it's written. It's definitely easier to learn than a third alphabet.

By popular demand, here is a comparison between the international phonetic alphabet, Arabic, English, and the system that is used in this book. The first three are non-standard letters you'll usually see in names or foreign words.

IPA	Arabic	As in..	This Book
p	پ	**p**ineapple	p
v	ڤ	**v**ictor	v
g	گ	**g**erkhin	g

IPA	Arabic	As in..	This Book
tˤ	ط	**T**all	T
d	د	**D**ead	d
dˤ	ض	**D**awn	D
Dʒ, g	ج	trea**s**ure	j
k	ك	**K**ong	k
f	ف	**F**elt	f
q	ق	cum**q**uat	q
ðˤ, zˤ	ظ	-	D
s	س	**S**afe	s
sˤ	ص	-	S
z	ز	**z**igguarat	z
ʃ	ش	**Sh**ame	sh
h	ه	**H**and	h
m	م	**M**end	m
n	ن	**N**ever	n
l	ل	**L**eaf	l
r	ر	**r**obocop	r
w	و	**W**eep	w
j	ي	**Y**urt	y
x	خ	Lo**ch**	kh
ɣ	غ	-	ghr
ħ	ح	-	H
ʕ	ع	-	3
ʔ	ء	**uh-oh**	'
iː	ي	**P**ee**p**	ee
i	unwritten	**P**it	e
æː, aː	ا	**g**rape	aa
æ, a	unwritten	**h**at	a
uː	و	**p**oop	oo
u	unwritten	**b**utt	u
eː	ي	**h**eel	ee
oː	و	**h**ope	o

Nouns

When it comes to nouns, there's actually not much to remember grammatically. Most of the work in using nouns comes from having to memorize them. In English, nouns do not have gender, and when a noun changes, adjectives associated with that noun usually don't. For example, in the phrase *that book is heavy* and *those books are heavy* the adjective is the same. That's not the case in darija.

There are four forms for each noun: male, female, male plural, and female plural. Any time that an adjective is used to describe one of these nouns, it has to agree with the noun in number and gender. Generally speaking, there are some trends in nouns:

- Any word ending in the *a* sound caused by a tamerbuta (ة) is feminine, however, masculine plurals sometimes end in tamerbutas just to confuse you;
- To create the feminine plural of a word, the tamerbuta becomes an *aat* sound (ات)
- Masculine nouns end in consonants
- The plural forms of nouns that have a long vowel near the end are made by removing that iong vowel

There are three kinds of nouns in Arabic:

Type I: No Inherent Gender

This type of noun has no inherent gender and can be male, female, or plural depending on how it is conjugated. For instance, the word for student:

Male	Taalib	طالب
Male Plural	Talaba	طلبة
Female	Taaliba	طالبة
Female Plural	Taalebaat	طالبات

A student has no inherent gender, however, specific students are associated with gender (my great grandfather Oakie is a Taleeb, his wife Zanie is a Taleeba, etc.) and therefore the words that are used to describe them are conjugated in that gender.

As Arabic has no concept of a genderless entity (it), anytime you are unsure of a person or object's gender, the male form is used. Also, groups containing both men and women are referred to by the male plural form, even if it is 300 women and 1 man, just like in French.

Type II: Inherent Gender

The other type of noun is one that has an inherent gender; it is either male or female. For instance, the word for *mother* (أم) is feminine (although it looks masculine because it does not end in a tamerbuta) and it should go without saying that masculine adjectives should not be used to describe someone's mother. This noun has only two forms: feminine singular and feminine plural, and there's no way to make it masculine.

Since adjectives and nouns must always agree in number and gender, this kind of noun is a little easier to work with, because feminine nouns will always require feminine adjectives, masculine nouns will always require masculine adjectives, and plural nouns of either gender will always require plural adjectives. For instance, a mother is always zweena (feminine pretty) and not zween (male pretty).

Type III: Dual Nouns

It should be noted that in classical Arabic there are two kinds of plural: dual and multiple. For instance, *two years* is not the same word as *year* or *three or more years*, and *two women* is not the same word as *three or more women*. In classical Arabic, all nouns have a dual form, but in darija, this form is only used for specific things (usually related to time).

For instance:

Day	yoom	يوم
Two days	yoomayn	يومين
Month	sh-harr	شهر
Two months	sh-hrayn	شهرين
Months	shoor/a	شهور \ ة
Year	3am	عام
Two years	3amayn	عامين
Years	sneen	سنين

Making the dual form of a noun just entails adding the sound *ayn* as a suffix. *Year* is also a good example of an irregular noun, where the plural form looks not even remotely anything like the singular form.

In darija, these are the only common words that use a dual form (aside from numbers containing a 2, such as 22, 32, 200, and 2000).

Independent Pronouns

Independent pronouns are used in almost every English sentence, usually to identify who is doing what. This is because English verbs are vague; the sentence "like hamburgers" doesn't tell the listener if it is I, you, we, or they that like hamburgers. In Moroccan Arabic, every verb is unique, so independent pronouns are only used in special situations.

I	ana	أنا
You (m. sing)	nta	نت
You (f. sing)	ntee	نت
He	hoowa	هو
She	heeya	هي
We	hnaa	حنا
You (pl.)	ntooma	نتما
They	hooma	هما

The words for 'you' referring to a male and 'you' referring to a female are spelled identically, because short vowels are not written in Arabic (except, of course, for in religious writing or writing meant for small children).

Independent pronouns are usually followed by a noun or adjective since the verb 'to be' is, as with many non-English languages, not necessary. *Mashee* (ماشي) is the word that is used on the occasion when one would want to negate a noun:

I am a student	ana talib	أنا طالب
I am not a student	ana mashee talib	أنا ماشي طالب
I am busy	ana mshghrool	أنا مشغول
I am not busy	ana mashee mshghrool	أنا ماشي مشغول
You are a professor	nta oosted	نت أستاد
You're not a professor!	nta mashee oosted!	نت ماشي أستاد

Object Pronouns

In English, independent pronouns are used to describe who is doing an action (such as *I* or *she*), while *object pronouns* are used to describe who is getting an action done to them (like *me* or *her*). For instance, in the sentence *I love her*, *I* is an independent pronoun and *her* is an object pronoun. In darija, the object pronouns are:

Me	nee	ـني
You (singular)	ek	ك
Him / It	oo / h	و/ ه
Her / It	ha	ها
Us	na	نا
You (plural)	kom	كم
Them	hom	هم

These object pronouns are the same as the possessive pronouns, with the exception of the word for *me*. In English, this would be as though the words *you* (object pronoun) and *your* (possessive pronoun) were the same word. Also, it should be noted that for the word *him*, و is used the majority of the time, the exceptions being when the verb already ends in a vowel.

In Arabic, object pronouns are attached to the end of a verb: they're not separate words like they are in English. For example:

Help me	awnnee	عاونّني
I love you	kanhbbek	كنحبّك
She loves me	kathbbeenee	كتحبّني
We frighten her	kankhwwfooha	كنخوّفوها
They tickled me	kayhrroonee	كيهرّوني
I will hit you	ghradee ndrbek	غادي نضربك

13

As you can see from the last two examples, the tense of the verb doesn't matter. Also, if the object pronoun is being used with a negative verb (i.e., something did not happen to someone) the negative prefix *ma* (ما) is added before the verb, and the negative suffix *sh* (ش) is added after the object pronoun (except in the future tense, just to mess with you):

I don't love her	makanhebbhash	ما كنحبّهاش
He doesn't fear me	makaykhaafneesh	ماكيخافنيش
We didn't see them	mashoofnaahumsh	ماشوفناهمش
I will not insult him	maghradeesh nsbboo	ماغاديش نسبّو

Possessive Pronouns

In Arabic, there are two ways to imply ownership of something: by using possessive pronouns and by using a form of the word *diyal*, (ديال), which means *of*. The possessive pronouns are:

My	ee	ي
Your (m or f)	ek	ك
His	oo	و
Her	ha	ها
Our	na	نا
Your (plural)	kom	كم
Their	hom	هم

Unlike English, these are not separate words in Arabic. Possessive pronouns are added to the noun as a suffix, making one word that implies ownership:

Book	ktab	كتاب
My book	ktabee	كتابي
Your book	ktabek	كتابك
His book	ktaboo	كتابو
Her book	ktabha	كتابها
Our book	ktabna	كتابنا
Your book	ktabkom	كتابكم
Their book	ktabhom	كتابهم

The second way to make a possessive involves the preposition ديال with a possessive suffix:

Of me (i.e., *my*)	dialee	ديالي
Of you (m or f)	dialek	ديالك
Of him	dialoo	ديالو

Of her	dialha	ديالها
Of us	dialna	ديالنا
Of you (pl)	dialkom	ديالكم
Of them	dialhom	ديالهم

These words are used with a noun that has a definite article (*the book* rather than just *book*):

My book	ktab dialee	الكتاب ديالي
Your book (m or f)	ktab dialek	الكتاب ديالك
His book	ktab dialoo	الكتاب ديالو
Her book	ktab dialha	الكتاب ديالها
Our book	ktab dialna	الكتاب ديالنا
Your book (pl)	ktab dialkom	الكتاب ديالكم
Their book	ktab dialhom	الكتاب ديالهم

Clearly, in English, the phrases *the book of me, the book of her,* etc. are not used very often; the examples above should be translated as *my book, her book,* and so on.

There is no difference in meaning between using a possessive pronoun or using ديال ; it's just a matter of taste as to which one is used.

Demonstrative Pronouns

Demonstrative pronouns (*this, that, these, those*) are used in the place of a proper noun. As with everything else in Arabic, they are gender-specific:

This (m)	hada	هدا
This (f)	hadee	هدي
This (pl)	hadoo	هدو
That (m)	hadak	هداك
That (f)	hadeek	هديك
Those (pl)	hadook	هدوك

Demonstrative pronouns are used as the subject of (or an object in) sentences:

That (f) is yellow	hadeek Sfr	هديك صفر
He ate that (m)	klaa hadak	كلى هداك

Demonstrative adjectives are similar, however, they describe a noun that is specifically included in a sentence. They are:

This/these (f, m, or pl)	had	هد
That (m)	dak	داك
That (f)	deek	ديك
Those	dook	دوك
This (situation)	had shee	هد شي
That (situation)	dak shee	داك شي

This book is good	had ktab mezian	هد كتاب مزيان
That couscous is spicy	dak ksksoo har	داك الكسكسو حار
I want that	bghreet dak shee	بغيت دك شي

17

Adjectives

In Arabic, adjectives must agree with the number and gender of the nouns that they modify, just like most languages other than English.

Every adjective has a masculine singular form. To get the feminine singular form of an adjective, simply add *a* (ة).

There are three different ways to make an adjective plural. The most common is to simply add *een* to the end of the word (ين). The second way is by replacing the long *ee* vowel (ي) with an *aa* (١) if it is found in the middle of the adjective. Generally speaking, every adjective that has ي *in the center of the word* is declined this way. If the ي is at the end of the adjective, it is declined in the first way.

These first two rules only cover making a masculine plural, for referring to a group of males or a mixed group of males and females. It is, however, possible to have a feminine plural to use when describing a group composed entirely of *the ladies*. This is done by removing the *een* ending from the plural masculine form and replacing it with *aat* (ات). Adjectives made plural in the second way discussed above (changing ي to ١) only have one plural form; it is the same regardless of the genders involved.

Finally, in Arabic, the adjective follows the noun, and *to be* isn't used:

He is ugly	huwa khayb	هو خايب
She is ugly	hiyya khayba	هي خايبة
They (masc) are ugly	homa khaybeen	هما خايبين
They (fem) are ugly	homa khaybaat	هما خايبات
He is old (lit.: big)	huwa kbeer	هو كبير
They (masc) are old	homa kbaar	هما كبار
They (fem) are old	homa kbaar	هما كبار

To negate an adjective, the word mashee (ماشي), is simply placed before the adjective, just like with nouns:

Pretty (m)	zween	زوين
Not pretty	ma-shee zween	ماشي زوين
I am not pretty	ana ma-shee zween	أنا ماشي زوين

Happy (f)	frhana	فرحانة
Not happy	ma-shee frhana	ماشي فرحانة
Sad/angry	mqllqa	مقلّقة
She is not happy	hiyya ma-shee frhana	هيّ ماشي فرحانة

Recall in the first example that, as a male, I use the male form of the adjective. If I was a woman, I would say *zweena*. In the second example, note that *not happy* might be a better way to describe someone's mood, since *sad* also means *angry*. Clearly, that doesn't happen all the time, but using *not* with adjectives is a quick way to double your vocabulary.

Comparative Adjectives

Comparative adjectives are used, of course, to compare things. For instance, *better* is the comparative form of *good*. There are actually a lot of irregular adjectives in Moroccan Arabic, unfortunately, it only becomes obvious that they are irregular when trying to use the comparative form.

To form the comparative of a regular adjective, simply remove the long *ee* (ي) from the masculine singular form. Also, in this context, the word *than* (as in, anchovies are tastier *than* pepperoni) is represented by the preposition *min* (من) :

He is older than she (is)	huwa kbr minha	هو كبر منها
I am heavy (said by man)	ana tqeel	أنا تقيل
I am heavier than you	ana tql minek	أنا تقل منك

Note that when using comparative adjectives as in "which pizza topping is better?" the word *ama* (أما) is used to mean "which" instead of *ashmin* (أشمن), which is used for "which is your pizza?" and so on.

For irregular adjectives, there's no way to know what the comparative form is going to be other than hearing a Moroccan say it. The more common irregular adjectives are:

Good / Better	mezian / Hsn	مزيان / حسن
Expensive/More expensive	ghralee/ghrlaa	غالي / غلى
Sweet / Sweeter	Hloo / Hlaa	حلو / حلى
Strong/Healthy	SHeeh/SHH	صحيح/صحّ

On the other hand, sometimes things just can't be compared. In a situation like this, one of two phrases is used to say "they're the same" (and are used as slang in France). These phrases are:

bhaal bhaal	بحال بحال
kif kif	كيف كيف

Superlative Adjectives

Superlative adjectives are used to describe *the most* or *the -est* of something. There are two choices for making an adjective superlative: Add the prefix *aa* to the beginning of the comparative form of the adjective or, more commonly, add a definite article to the adjective and a personal pronoun into the sentence. For example:

She is the nicest	heeya DDreefa	هي الضريفة
(Literally: she is the nice!)		
He is the busiest	huwa lmshghrool	هو المشغول
(Literally: he is the busy)		

Be sure to remember that when making an adjective superlative, it still has to agree with the noun it is modifying in terms of gender and number.

He is the most expensive	huwa ghla	هو أغلى
(This would be said about a masculine noun)		
She is the shortest	heya qssar	هي قصر
God is the biggest[1]	allahu aakbar	الله أكبر

Unlike Classical Arabic, in darija, pronouns wouldn't normally be used like this. If it's not clear who is being talked about the name would be used (i.e. Anthony is the hungriest); if it is clear, just the adjective would be used and the pronoun is understood. Pronouns are written above just to show they agree with the adjectives.

---

[1] Said during the call to prayer; 'biggest' is meant in the sense of 'greatest' or 'most grand'. 'Biggest' is a literal and, in this case, insufficient translation.

Verbs from Adjectives

In English, it is not always possible to make a verb out of an adjective. For instance, the meaning of *I am cold* is clear, but *I cold* doesn't make as much sense. In Arabic, however, this is easy to do by removing the center vowels of adjectives. They are then declined as normal verbs and can be translated as, for example, *to be cold*:

Cold (adjective)	bared	بارد
To be cold (verb)	brd	برد
I am cold (via adjective)	ana bared	أنا بارد
I am cold (via verb)	kanbrd	كنبرد

Verbs are discussed in the next section. There's not really any difference in meaning, and which form you choose to use is a matter of preference and region. Some more examples:

Warm (adjective)	daafee	دافي
To be warm	dfee	دفي
I am warm (w/ adjective)	ana daafee	أنا دافي
I am warm (w/ verb)	kandfa	كندفا
Fear (adjective)	khayef	خايف
To be afraid	khaaf	خاف
I am afraid (w/ adjective)	ana khayef	أنا خايف
I am afraid (w/ verb)	kankhaaf	كنخاف

Note that this doesn't work all the time. There are plenty of irregular adjectives:

Hungry (adjective)	jee3aan	جيعان
To be hungry (infinitive)	jaa3	جاع
I am hungry (w/ adjective)	ana je3aan	أنا جيعان
I am hungry (w/ verb)	kanjoo3	كنجوع

The Nisba

The word *nisba* in classical Arabic refers to an adjective that has been created from a noun – generally an adjective that describes a person with some relation to whatever the noun is. Normally, a nisba is identifiable by the sound *ee* on the end; in fact, one of the first things students of darija learn is a noun-nisba pairing:

Morocco	lmaghreb	المغرب	(noun)
Moroccan	maghrebee	مغربي	(nisba)
Fes	faas	فاس	(noun)
Fassi	faassee	فاسي	(nisba)

In this case, the noun in question is the name of the country of Morocco (or the city of Fes). The nisba of this noun is formed simply by adding an *ee* sound and refers to a person with some relation to Morocco; specifically, a person (or object) from Morocco or Fes.

Type I: Irregular – *wee* suffix

There are several types of irregular nisba. With nouns that end in an *a* sound, adding a long vowel would not sound good, so a *w* sound is added before the suffix. This is almost always true of monosyllable words:

France	fransa	فرنسا	(noun)
French	fransawee	فرنساوي	(nisba)
Sla (a city)	sla	سلا	(noun)
From Sla	slawee	سلاي	(nisba)

Type II: Irregular – *nee* suffix

The majority of nouns that end in an *a* sound have a *wee* suffix as shown above rather than just *ee*. There are, however, some exceptions, where the *nee* sound is added instead. Also, nouns that end in consonants will occasionally have *a nee* as a suffix, rather than just plain *ee*:

desire/greed	shewa	شوا
greedy person	shewanee	شواني
foreign	berra	برّا
foreigner	berranee	برّاني

Type III: Irregular – *a* dropped

Sometimes, words that end in an *a* sound choose to just drop the *a* altogether and replace it, rather than add an consonant between *a* and *ee*:

coffee	qahwa	قهوة
coffee-colored	qahwee	قهوي

This is for the best, because "qahwawee" sounds really strange.

Type IV: Irregular – no set pattern

There are, of course, some words that refuse to play by the rules and don't fit into any category or pattern. For example:

Spain	sbaanya	سبانيا
Spanish	sblyoonee	سبليوني

This word is just a mess. Sure, an *ee* sound is added at the end (but, like the word for *French*, without a *w*); an *L* sound is inserted near the beginning; the *aa* vowel sound changes to *oo*; and the *y* has been disposed of. Some words just can't be categorized and go into the "very irregular" bin.

Above, the rules for making a nisba have been covered. However, there are different categories of words from which nisbas can be made:

From Singular Nouns

It makes sense that if a nisba is an adjective made out of a noun, the first category of nisba would be those made from singular nouns. For example:

Religion	deen	دين
Religious	deenee	ديني
Honey	3sl	عسل
Honey-colored	3sslee	عسلي
Hotel	fondooq	فندق
Hotel keeper	fondooqee	فندقي
Newspaper	gazetta	گازطة
Newspaper Vendor	gwaztee	گوازتي

From Participles of Spatial Relations

Words that refer to relative positions all have nisbas:

Outside	berra	برّا
Stranger/exterior	berranee	برّاني
Inside	dakhel	داخل
Internal	dakhelanee	داخلاني
Above	fuq	فوق
Upper	fuqaanee	فوقاني
The Rear	lerr	لرّ
Rear/hindmost	lerranee	لرّاني
Facing	qoddam	قدّام
Lying ahead	qoddamee	قدّامي
Below/Under	teht	تحت
Beneath	tehtanee	تحتني
Behind/After	werra	ورا
Last	werranee	وراني
Middle/Center	wost	وسط
Middle/Central	wostanee	وسطاني

25

From Numbers

The numbers three through ten all have nisbas, which take on the general meaning of composed of three elements, three sided, or three-fold:

Three	tlaata	تلاتة
Three-fold	tlaatee	تلاتي
Four	(a)rb3a[2]	(أ)ربعة
Four-fold	arbaaee	رباعي
Five	khamsa	خمسة
Five-fold	khamsee	خماسي
Six	staa	ستّة
Six-fold	sdaasee	سداسي
Seven	sbaa	سبعة
Seven-fold	sbaa3ee	سباعي
Eight	timineeya	تمنية
Eight-Fold	tmanee	تماني
Nine	ts3ood	تسعود
Nine-fold	tsa3ee	تساعي
Ten	3ashra	عشرة
Ten-fold	3sharee	عشاري

From Place Names

Pretty much every location has a nisba, which translates as "a person from _____" or an "inhabitant of _____." It is also used to describe objects from these places.

India	l'hnd	ال هند
Indian	hindee	هندي
Rabat	rrbaat	الرباط
Rabatian	rabatee	رباطي

---

[2] The 'a' in parenthesis may be omitted, depending on your location .

Tunisia	toons	تونس
Tunisian	toonsee	تونسي
Syria	sham	الشّام
Syrian	shaamee	شامي

For the record, the name 'shaam' for 'Syria' is archaic. It's included here to appeal to the retro vintage crowd. The modern form is "Surya" and its nisba is "suryee" (سوري and سوريا).

From Colors

When nisbas of certain nouns are made, they take on the meaning of " –colored". For instance, 'gray' literally translates to 'ash-colored':

Sulphur	kebrit	كبريت
Light yellow	kebritee	كبريتي
Apricot	mishmash	مشماش
Apricot colored	mishmaashee	مشماشي
Ashes	rmaad	رماد
Ash colored (gray)	rmaadee	رمادي
Honey	3sl	عسل
Honey-colored	3sslee	عسلي
Gold	dheb	دهب
Golden	dhebee	دهبي

From Professional or Personal Characteristics

For any noun that describes a profession, a nisba can be made which generally translates as "a ____maker", "a ____seller", or "a ____ merchant".

Book	ktab	كتاب
Bookseller	ktobee	كتبي
Chicken	djaaj	دجاج
Chicken merchant	djaajee	دجايجي

Silver	nqraa	نقرا
Silversmith	nqayree	نقايري
Comb	meshta	مشتة
Comb-maker	meshaytee	مشايتي
Satchel	shkaara	شكرة
Bag-maker	shkaayree	شكايري
Boat	flooka	فلوكة
Boatman	flaykee	فلايكي
Salt-mine	mellaha	ملحة
Salt-miner	mlalhee	ملالحي
Party	zerda	زردة
Glutton	zraydee	زرايدي

Verbs

Before learning how to conjugate verbs, it's probably best to look at their structure. There are four kinds of verbs. The regular kind is conjugated by normal rules in the past, present, and future. Two kinds of irregular verbs require some sort of modification during conjugation (i.e. the insertion or removal of letters) and one kind of irregular verb requires modification in the past tense, but not in the present. How to work with these verbs will be discussed in the chapters covering the various tenses; this is just a short overview of the different kinds of verbs. Many of these rules are similar to the ones found in classical Arabic.

Regular Verbs

Regular verbs are the easiest to deal with because *they don't contain long vowels in the final or middle positions.* There are two kinds of regular verbs. The first are verbs with only three letters:

To know	3rf	عرف
To understand	fhem	فهم

Regular verbs do not contain long vowels in the final or middle positions. The second kind of regular verb is one with more than three letters. For example:

To speak	tekellem	تكلّم
To travel	saafer	سافر

Notice that that last one, *to travel,* has a long vowel in it, but it is not in the middle or final position.

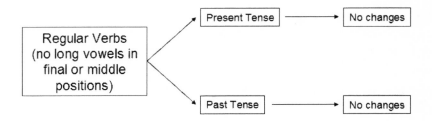

Type I: Irregular Verbs – Long Vowel in Final Position

The first type of irregular verb has a long vowel in the final position. This raises a number of problems, because verbs are conjugated in darija through the use of both prefixes (in the present) and suffixes (in the past, or for females and plurals). For example, قرى (qraa) means *to study* or *to read*.

If this word were to be conjugated simply by adding a suffix, there would be a lot of confusion in the past tense, as "I studied" and "she studied" would be the same. Since Arabic so rarely uses pronouns, this would make a big mess.

When learning a Type I irregular verb, two forms must be remembered: the infinitive (for use in the past) and the present.

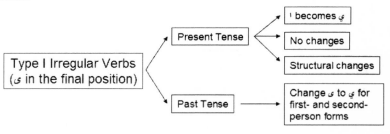

Type II: Irregular Verbs – Long Vowel in Middle Position

Of course, if verbs don't start with long vowels, and the first type of irregular verb has a long vowel at the end, the second kind must be a verb with a long vowel in the middle. For example, شاف (shaaf) is the infinitive of the verb *to see*.

30

To conjugate this verb in the past, vowels are removed some of the time; to conjugate it in the present, vowels change (or not) some of the time. So they are probably the most difficult verbs to use.

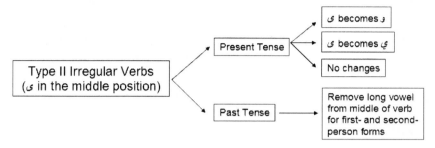

Type III: Irregular Verbs – Two Letter Verbs

These verbs are the product of an exotic grammatical concept in Arabic: the shedda. The shedda is sort of like a punctuation mark, and when it appears above a letter, it means that letter ought to appear twice. For instance:

To think   dnn   ظنّ (instead of ظنن)

These verbs are irregular in the past tense and require the insertion of vowels to break up long string of consonants. However, in the present tense they are regular and follow normal rules of conjugation.

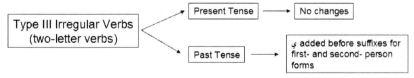

Because irregular verbs have different verb stems in the past and present tenses, this overview treats both tenses simultaneously. First the general rules of the tenses are given, then how to form verb stems for the types of irregular verbs are reviewed. Finally, how to use more than one verb in a sentence is discussed.

Present and Past Tenses

The Present Habitual Tense – Introduction

Verbs are conjugated in the present tense by adding prefixes, and sometimes suffixes, to the verb. Prefixes depend on the person of the verb; suffixes depend on whether the verb is plural or feminine. Therefore, *I* and *we*, which are both in the first person, have the same prefix, but because *we* is plural, it also has a suffix:

I	kan_____		كن_____
You (m)	kat_____		كت_____
You (f)	kat_____	ee	كت_____ي
He	kay_____		كي_____
She	kat_____		كت_____
We	kan_____	oo	كن_____و
You (pl)	kat_____	oo	كت_____و
They	kay_____	oo	كي_____و

The prefixes don't really have an equivalent in English and are actually the participle of the verb *to be* (explained below). They are not usually said by theirselves in the present, but are combined with the verb as shown here. This construction conveys four pieces of information: that the action is in the present tense (ka-) the person of the action (-n, -t, or -y) the plurality/gender of the person doing the action (-ee or -oo) as well as the action (whatever the verb is). For instance:

You (m) drink	katshreb	كتشرب
You (f) drink	katshrebee	كتشربي
You (pl) drink	katshreboo	كتشربو

This is the manner in which the present tense is formed regardless of whether the verb is regular or irregular. The only hurdle to overcome is knowing exactly how to conjugate the verb from the imperative (the third person past) to the present stem. Finally, this tense refers to habitual action; the examples above refer to repeated actions (i.e. *I usually drink milk* or *I drink mint tea every Thursday.*)

The Past Tense – Introduction

The simple past tense is formed simply by adding suffixes to the verb stem. The third-person masculine form (he) is not changed, and is simply the verb stem. Further, the male and female singular forms are identical:

I	____t	ت____
You (m)	____tee	تي____
You (f)	____tee	تي____
He		
She	____at	ات____
We	____na	نا____
You (pl)	____too	تو____
They	____oo	و____

To drink is regular and can be conjugated in the past:

I drank	shrebt	شربت
You (m or f) drank	shrebtee	شربتي
He drank	shreb	شرب
They drank	shreboo	شربو

This is the "simple past" and refers to an action that occurred, and was completed, in the past.

Verb Stem Formation: Regular

Regular verbs require no changes in both the present and past tenses. As seen above, the verb stem for *to drink* is the same in the past and present, and requires only the addition of suffixes and/or prefixes to be conjugated. Here is another example, using the regular verb *to travel* (سافر):

I usually travel	kansafr	كنسافر
I traveled	safrt	سافرت
He usually travels	kaysafr	كيسافر
He traveled	safr	سافر
We usually travel	kansafroo	كنسافرو
We traveled	safrna	سافرنا

Verb Stem Formation: Type I Irregular

Type I irregular verbs end with an ى (aa sound). In the past tense, this vowel is simply removed in some forms, whereas in the present tense it changes to a different vowel. To conjugate a type I irregular verb in the past, the ى is changed into an ي for the first- and second- person (*I, you (m, f, or pl)*, and *we*) before the past tense endings are added. For instance, the verb *to go* is *mshaa* (stem: مشى):

I went	msheet	مشيت
You (m or f) went	msheetee	مشيتي
He went	mshaa	مشى
She went	mshaat	مشات
We went	msheena	مشينا
You (pl) went	msheetoo	مشيتو
They went	mshaaw	مشاو

Notice that for the *she* form, only the "t" sound is added, rather than "at". This is to avoid forming some fairly unpleasant sounds, such as mshaaat.

In the present tense, things are a little more complicated. This is because to form the stem, the ى sound changes. There are three manners in which it can be changed: the ى can change

34

into an ي, it can change the interior of the verb, or it can remain an ى.

ى remains ى verbs are conjugated like a regular verb, with the present tense prefixes and suffixes being added to the verb stem. For example, قرى is the stem of *to read* or *to study*:

I study	kanqraa	كنقرا
You (m) study	katqraa	كتقرا
You (f) study	katqraay	كتقراي
She studies	katqraa	كتقرا
He studies	kayqraa	كيفــــرى
We study	kanqraw	كنقراو
You (pl) study	katqraw	كتقراو
They study	kayqraw	كيقراو

In the north of Morocco the female second person verb doesn't take an –aay ending. That is, it's pronounced the same as the male second person (both are, above, katqraa).

ى becomes ي verbs are treated the same way, after changing the vowel. For instance, مشى means *to go*. In the present tense, the final vowel becomes an ي:

I am going	kanmshee	كنمشي
You are going (m or f)	katmshee	كتمشي
She is going	katmshee	كتمشي
He is going	kaymshee	كيمشي
We are going	kanmsheew	كنمشيو
You (pl) are going	katmsheew	كتمشيو
They are going	kaymsheew	كيمشيو

Technically, this conjugation refers to a habitual action: *I usually go*, etc. Notice that in this case, the male and female singular forms are the same (as compared to the present tense of regular verbs, where the female singular also has a suffix).

There are only two Type I irregular verbs that see internal changes when conjugated in the present tense: *to eat* (كلى) and *to take* (خدى). These verbs move the vowel from the end to the beginning of the verb:

I eat	kanakul	كناكل
You (m) eat	katakul	كتاكل
You (f) eat	kataklee	كتاكلي
She eats	katakul	كتاكل
He eats	kayakul	كياكل
We eat	kanakloo	كناكلو
You (pl) eat	katakloo	كتاكلو
They eat	kayakloo	كياكلو

Verb Stem Formation: Type II Irregular

Type II irregular verbs have an ى in their middle positions. They are relatively easy to conjugate in the past tense: the vowel is simply removed in the first- and second-person forms, and then the suffixes are added. As above, only a *t* sound, and not an *aat* sound, are added to the *she* form. Shaaf (شاف) is the stem of the verb *to see*:

I saw	shft	شفت
You (m or f)	sawshftee	شفتي
She saw	shaft	شافت
He saw	shaaf	شاف
We saw	shfna	شفنا
You (pl) saw	shftoo	شفتو
They saw	shafoo	شافو

36

In the present tense, the story is again more complicated: the ى can change into an و, an ي, or remain an ى, depending on the verb.

For verbs that do not change the stem, the present tense suffixes and prefixes are simply added to the verb stem. خاف means *to fear*:

I fear	kankhaaf	كنخاف
You (f) fear	katkhaafee	كتخافي
You (m) fear	katkhaaf	كتخاف
She fears	katkhaaf	كتخاف
He fears	kaykhaaf	كيخاف
We fear	kankhaafoo	كنخافو
You (pl) fear	katkhaafoo	كتخافو
They fear	kaykhafoo	كيخافو

Verbs that change the final vowel, whether it is to و or ي are treated the same way after this change occurs. As mentioned above, شاف means *to see*:

I see	kanshoof	كنشوف
You (f) see	katshoofee	كتشوفي
You (m) see	katshoof	كتشوف
She sees	katshoof	كتشوف
He sees	kayshoof	كيشوف
We see	kanshoofoo	كنشوفو
You (pl) see	katshoofoo	كتشوفو
They see	kayshoofoo	كيشوفو

Verb Stem Formation: Type III Irregular

Type III verbs are the "two letter" verbs that contain a shedda. In the past tense, they require only the addition of an ي

37

to the first- and second- person forms before the past tense suffixes are added. ظَنّ means *to think*:

I thought	Dhnneet	ظنّيت
You (f) thought	Dhnneetee	ظنّيتي
You (m) thought	Dhnneetee	ظنّيتي
She thought	Dhnnat	ظنّات
He thought	Dhnn	ظنّ
We thought	Dhnneena	ظنّينا
You (pl) thought	Dhnneetoo	ظنّيتو
They thought	Dhnnoo	ظنّو

These verbs, in the present tense, are regular and require only the addition of the present tense prefixes and suffixes.

Negating Verbs

To negate a verb in any tense, both a prefix *ma* (ما) and suffix *sh* (ش) are usually used:

I know	kan3arf	كنعرف
I do not know	ma kan3rf sh	ماكنعرفش
I knew	3arft	عرفت
I did not know	ma3arftsh	ماعرفتش

A small handful of verbs do not require a suffix under certain conditions. These verbs use either just the prefix *ma* or the prefix *maat*. These verbs are usually irregular and are discussed in more detail in their own sections. Some examples:

To not be pleased by (something) – (عجب)

| I don't like (her, you, it) | makat3jbnish | ماكتعجبنيش |

Nothing - (حتّى حاجة , والو)

| I knew nothing | ma3rft waaloo | ماعرفت والو |
| I knew nothing | ma3rft htta haja | ماعرفت حتّى حاجة |

No one - (حتّى واحد)

| I knew no one | ma3rft htta wahed | ماعرفت حتّى واحد |

Neither, nor (with nouns) – (لا ... ولا)
I knew neither him nor her
ma3rft la huwa wla hiyya
ماعرفت لا هو ولا هي

Neither, nor (with verbs) – (ما...ما)
I neither eat nor drink
makanakool makanshreb
ماكنكول ماكنشرب

To still don't / To not yet – (مازال ما)
I am not yet married
mazal ma mzzwjsh
مازال ما مزوّجش

To never have done – (ما عمرّي)
I have never eaten that
ma 3mree kleetoo
ما عمرّي كليتو

Without (doing something) – (بلا ما...)
Without eating, I will die
eelaa ma kleetsh, ghradee nmoot
إيلا ماكليتش غادي نموت

It's been a long time since – (هاذي شحال ما...)
It's been a long time since I ate
hadhe sh'haal makleet
هاذي شحال ماكليت

Only – (غير)
I speak only English
makantkellem gheer lengleeziya
ماكنتكلّم غير النڭليزية

Multiple Verb Use

It's normal to use two verbs in one sentence. For instance, that previous sentence is a two-verb sentence: "It is...to use." In English, the second verb is usually the infinitive, as in "I hate to dance" or "He sings to anger me."

In Arabic, the second verb is in a shortened version of the present tense, rather than the infinitive. It is made by dropping the 'ka' sound. This is done whether there are two, three, or four hundred verbs in a sentence (not that 400-verb sentences come up often in conversation). For instance:

كنبغي ناكول
kanbghree nakool
I like to eat
(instead of kanbghree *ka*nakool)

كنحاول نتعلّم نتكلّم ب الدارجة المغربية
kanhaawl nt3allem ntkellem b darija lmaghrebeyya
I am trying to learn to speak the Moroccan dialect

حاول يقبطني !
haawl yqbTnee!
He tried to grab me!

غادي نحاول نتجنّب نتكرّع
ghradee nhaawl ntjnnb ntgrra3
Literally: I will to try to avoid to burp
Meaning: I will try to avoid burping

To burp contains a letter (*G*) that doesn't exist in Classical Arabic. In darija, however, it's a perfectly fine letter, borrowed mainly from Egyptian words. There are other non-standard letters (such as *V or P*) that don't exist in either Classical or Moroccan and were introduced to accommodate foreign sounds. These letters are usually avoided in this book, and in general are only found in foreign names or technical words.

The Imperative Tense

Another way to conjugate verbs in the present tense is to order someone to do something. Or, to tell someone very specifically not to do something. Fortunately, the imperative is simple because there are only three kinds: the male, female, and plural versions of *you*. One would say *Hey you! Go to the store!* But the phrase *Hey I! Go to the store!* or *Hey they! Go to the store!* makes no sense. Just to make it *really* obvious, the phrase 'Hey you!' is used to denote the imperative here.

The imperative is formed by dropping the prefix from the present habitual tense:

You (male) drink	katshreb	كتشرب
You (female) drink	katshrebee	كتشربي
You (plural) drink	katshreboo	كتشربو
Hey you (male)!	Drink! shreb!	شرب
Hey you (female)!	Drink! shrebee!	شربي
Hey you (pl)!	Drink! shreboo!	شربو

Stop, in the name of love!
wqf, bism lHubb!
وقف بسم الحبّ

To negate the imperative, that is, to tell someone not to do something, is almost the same as negating a verb in the present tense, but not quite. The letter ت is added to the end of the prefix; the suffix stays the same. For instance:

(To m) Don't drink!	mat-shrebsh!	ماتشربش
(To fem.) Don't drink!	mat-shrebeesh!	ماتشربيش
(To pl.) Don't drink!	mat-shreboosh!	ماتشربوش

The Future Tense

In English, the phrases *I am going to eat* and *I will eat* mean the same thing in everyday conversation. For the vast majority of people, which one they use is just a question of taste (pun intended).

In Arabic, there is only one way to form the future tense. The word غادي (ghradi) is inserted before the verb. For the future tense, the verb is conjugated in the present, however, since غادي is treated like a verb meaning *going to*, it is the second verb in the sentence and is treated accordingly. For more information on using multiple verbs in the same sentence, see the section on the present tense. For example:

I am going to drink	ghradi nshreb	غادي نشرب
You (m) are going to drink	ghradi tshreb	غادي تشرب
You (f) are going to drink	ghradi tshrebee	غادي تشربي
He is going to drink	ghradi yshreb	غادي يشرب
She is going to drink	ghradi tshreb	غادي تشرب
We are going to drink	ghradi nshreboo	غادي نشربو
You (pl) are going to drink	ghradi tshreboo	غادي تشربو
They are going to drink	ghradi yshreboo	غادي يشربو

While either *going to drink* or *will drink* are acceptable translations, the former was used here to reiterate the fact that whatever the action is (in this case *to drink*) is treated as the second verb in the phrase. Also, in the north of Morocco the verb *mshaa* (مشا) is used instead of ghradi. This verb <u>literally</u> means *to go* as in *we should go to the theatre*. In the south, *ghradi* is much preferred.

In Arabic, every word must be conjugated to agree with the rest of the sentence in terms of gender and number; the future tense is no exception. Instead of غادي, it is not unusual to see غادية or غاديين (*ghradeeya* or *ghradee-een*) for female and plural phrases, respectively. Additionally, instead of using the whole word غادي, the single-letter prefix غ is sometime used for people speaking or writing quickly. When this happens, the verb is still treated as the second verb in the sentence and the single-letter prefix still applies. Examples of these three oddities:

She is going to drink	ghradia tshreb	غادية تشرب
They're going to drink	ghradieen yshreboo	غاديين يشربو
I'm going to drink	ghrashreb	غانشرب

As can be seen, the future tense is as easy as eating pancakes, as long as you know how to conjugate the verb in the present tense. Negating the future tense is also easy: the same prefix and suffix that are used with other verbs (ما...ش) are placed on غادي to form to give *maghradeesh*, ماغاديش, which translates as *not going to*.

غادي can also be followed by a location. If this is done, it has the same meaning as in English: *I am going to (someplace)*. For example:

I am going to the souk
ghradee lsooq
غادي السوق

We are going to go to Fes
ghradee faas
غادي فاس

The Past Progressive / Past Habitual Tense

The *Past Progressive* is also referred to as the *Past Continuous* tense. This tense expresses something that happened in the past, but only for a span of time, as in *I was doing something* rather than *I did something*. It is made with *to be* in the past tense followed by a second verb in the present:

I was sleeping	kunt na3s	كنت ناعس
He was talking	kaan kaytekellem	كان كيتكلّم
We were working	kunnaa kankhdemoo	كنّا كنخدمو

At this point in my Moroccan Arabic studies, I felt very badly lied to. It turns out that there's a verb 'to be'! Perhaps it should have been mentioned before, more explicitly, but it really never came up. Regardless, this portion of the book is an overview of how to make verb tenses; to find more information on specifically how to conjugate 'to be', kindly turn to the section below on Special Verbs, right after the discussion of verb participles. One important thing to note now, however, is how similar the verb 'to be' (kunt, kaan, kunna) is to the prefixes used to make the present tense (kan, kat, etc.)

Much more commonly this tense is used a little bit differently, with the verb *to be* in the past and the verb in the present, and is translated in the sense of *used to do something*:

I used to sleep	kunt kann3s	كنت كننعس
He used to talk	kaan kaytekellem	كان كيتكلّم
We used to work	kunnaa kankhdemoo	كنّا كنخدمو

When I was small, I used to read every day
melli kunt sghreer, kunt kanqraa kull nhaar
ملّي كنت صغير كنت كنقرا كلّ نهار

I was going to the medina when she saw me
kunt mashee L lmedina melli shaaftni
كنت ماشي ل المدينة ملّي شافتني

When I arrived at the train station, the train was just leaving
mlli wslt L la gaar,l'mashina kaant katkhrj / traan kaan
kaykhrej
ملّي وصلت ل لا گار المشينة كانت كتخرج / ملي تران كان كيخرج

(While we're on the subject of trains, *l'gaar* comes from French and is used specifically to refer to a train station. *l'mashina* is used to refer to a station of any sort, whether it's for buses, trains, or zepplins. *L'mashina* is also what's known as 'country' dialect and when you use it people might laugh – but at least you'll be understood. It's a little like saying 'pop' instead of 'soda' in the USA. The more modern word *tran* is used in the north of Morocco, and *traan* can be heard elsewhere. Did I mention that Moroccan Arabic varies a lot?)

One use of the Past Progressive tense is to refer to intended actions that did not become fulfilled. In darija, this is made by using *to be* in the past tense followed by a second verb in the future tense; it translates literally as *was going to* and figuratively as *had intended to*:

He was going to sing
kaan ghradee yghrennee
كان غادي يغنّي
(He had intended to sing)

I was going to live in Fes
kunt ghradee nskun f fass
كنت غادي نعيش ف فاس
(I had intended to live in Fes)

Clearly, these short examples don't really make much sense on their own. This type of sentence almost always demands the word *but* in it, to explain why the action went unfulfilled:

I was going to live in fes, but I had no money
kunt ghradee nskun f fass, walakeen ma kaanush 3andee lfloos
كنت غادي نسكن ف فاس و لاكن ما كانوش عندي الفلوس

He was going to see me, but he was tired
kaan ghradee yshoofni, wa laaken kaan 3ayyaan
كان غادي يشوفني و لاكن كان عيّان

We were going to write, but did not have time
kn-naa ghradee nktboo, wa laaken ma kaansh 3andhnaa lwaqt
كننا غادي نكتبو و لاكن ما كانش عندنا الوقت

But is not used for negative intentions, that is, something that one did not intend to do. For these, *to be* is conjugated in the past, negated, and the second verb is in the future tense:

I was not going to push you!
makuntsh ghradee ndf3k!
ماكنتش غادي ندفعك

He was not going to pay her.
makaansh ghradee ykhllS'ha
ماكانش غادي يخلّصها

We were not going to eat the couscous.
makn-naash ghradee nakloo ksksoo
ماكنناش غادي ناكلو الكسكسو

The Past Perfect

The Past Perfect is used to refer to things that occurred in the past, before something else occurred. For instance, *we had eaten* implies that at some point in the past we had finished eating, but by itself, this phrase isn't a complete sentence. The other event that occurred needs to be known for this phrase to express a complete thought.

It is made by using the past tense of *to be* followed by another verb in the past tense:

We had eaten	kn-naa kleenaa	كنّا كلينا
They had left	kaannoo khrjoo	كانو خرجو
He had died	kaan maat	كان مات

When I arrived at the station, the train had left
mlli wslt L la gaar, l'mashina kaant khrjt
ملّي وصلت ل لا گار المشينة كانت خرجت

We had cooked the food before we ate it
kn-naa tybna lmakla 3ad kleenaha
كنّا طيّبنا المكلا عاد كلينها

I cried because she had hurt me
bkeet 3lahaqqash kaant Drrtnee
بكيت الاحقاش كانت ضرّتني

48

The Present Perfect Progressive

The Present Perfect Progressive tense describes things that began to occur in the past and have continued to the present. For instance, *I have been eating since noon* implies that I began eating at noon, and am currently eating. The same with *I have not eaten since Thursday*. I started not eating on Thursday, and I'm still not eating.

There are a number of different ways to form this tense. Further, this tense is frequently used as part of a question/answer session, so both how to phrase the question and how to reply for five different ways are given below:

1) Q: How long have you been <u>verb</u> ing?
   sh'Haal hadee w <u>present</u>?
   شحال هادي و ــــــــ؟

A: I have been <u>verb</u> ing for <u>time</u>.
   hadee <u>time</u> w <u>present tense</u>.
   هادي ــــــــ و ــــــــ.

How long have you been singing?
sh'Haal hadee wnta katghrennee?
شحال هادي ونت كتغنّي؟

I have been singing for two weeks.
hadee jooj semanat wanakanghrenee.
هادي جوج سيمانات ونا كنغنّي.

2) Q: Since when has <u>name</u> <u>verb</u> ed?
   mn foqaash w <u>name</u> <u>present tense</u>?
   من فوقاش و ــــــــ ــــــــ؟

A: Since <u>time</u>, <u>name</u> <u>present tense</u>.
   mn <u>time</u> w <u>name</u> <u>present tense</u>.
   من ــــــــ و ــــــــ ــــــــ.

Since when has Bob cooked?
mn foqaash w Bob kayTyyb?
من فوقاش و بوب كيطيّب؟

Bob has cooked for two weeks.
haadi jooj semanat w Bob kayTyyb
هادي جوج سيمانات و بوب كيطيّب.

3) Q:How long ago did you <u>past tense</u>?
sh'Haal hadee baash <u>past tense</u>?
شحال هادي باش ـــــــ؟

A: It has been <u>time</u> since I <u>past tense</u>.
hadee <u>time</u> baash <u>past tense</u>.
هادي ـــــ باش ـــــ.

How long ago did you eat?
sh'Haal hadee baash kleetee?
شحال هادي باش كليتي؟

I ate two weeks ago.
hadee jooj semanat baash kleet.
هادي جوج سيمانات باش كليت.

4) Q: How long since one <u>verb</u> ed?
sh'Haal hadee ma <u>past tense</u>?
شحال هادي ما ـــــ؟

A: It has been <u>time</u> since <u>past tense</u>.
hadee <u>time</u> ma <u>past tense</u>.
هادي ـــــ ما ـــــ.

How long since you ate?
sh'Haal hadee ma kleetee?
شحال هادي ما كليتي؟

It has been a long time since I ate.
hadee mooda ma kleet.

هادي مدة ما كليت.

5) Q: Since when have you not <u>verb</u>?
mn foqaash ma <u>past tense</u>?

من فوقاش ما ـــــــ؟

A: Since <u>time,</u> I have not <u>past tense</u>.
mn <u>time</u>, ma <u>past tense</u>.

من ـــــــ ما ـــــــ.

Q: Since when have you not smoked?
mn foqash ma kmeetee?

من فوقاش ما كميتي؟

A: I have not smoked for two weeks.
haadee jooj semanat ma kmeet.

هادي جوج سيمانات ما كميت.

The first version is for saying that one has been doing something *for* a certain amount of time, and the second one is for saying that one has been doing something *since* a certain time. Versions three, four, and five all refer to something that happened (or did not happen) in the past and, in the present, these actions are *continuing* to happen. Or not happen, as in version five.

Future Perfect / Future Perfect Continuous

The Future Perfect tense describes something that will occur in the future, but only for a limited span of time. For instance, *I will have eaten this hoagie before nine o'clock*. It's in the future, and it will take some amount of time, but I'll be done by 9:00. In English, this tense is always identifiable by some variant of *will have....* In darija, this tense is made by combining the future, present, and past tenses:

ghradee (*to be* in the present tense) (verb in past tense)

Each of these words must agree with gender, number, and person. For example:

I will have eaten it
ghadee nkoon kleetoo
غادي نكون كليتو
(literally: I am going to I was I ate him)

He will have heard
ghadee ykoon sma3
غادي يكون سمع
(literally: he is going to he was to hear)

The Future Perfect Continuous tense, on the other hand, refers to an event that will occur in the future for an indefinite span of time. For instance, *at nine o'clock I will have been waiting for two hours*. The future perfect continuous, in English, is always identifiable by some variant of *will have been....* In Arabic, the Future Perfect Continuous is just like Future Perfect, except the final verb is in the present continuous, not the past:

ghadee (to be in the present) (verb in present continuous)

For example:

I will have been living here

ghadee nkoon kanskun hnaa

غادي نكون كنسكن هنا

(literally: I am going to I was I am living here)

We will have been eating for an hour

ghradee nkoonoo shee saa3a w Hnaa kanakloo

غادي نكونو شي ساعة وحنا كنكلو

(literally: we are going to we were we are eating an hour)

It doesn't sound as weird if you try not to translate it word-for-word. Seriously. Don't do that.

The Conditional Tense

As the name implies, the conditional tense is used to indicate that a condition must be met before some action can occur. Naturally, there are two different outcomes: either the condition can be (or was) met, and therefore the action is possible, or the condition cannot be (or was not) met and therefore the action is impossible.

The first kind of sentence, which indicates that the action is possible, cannot be translated sensibly word-for-word into English, because the first verb is usually in the past tense. This sort of sentence uses 'eela', the word *if* (إلا).

The second type of sentence is recognizable by the words lokan,... lokan (لوكان ... لوكان), which in darija is used to mean *if I had ... I would have* and replaces the word *if*. Folks from Casablanca use كون instead of لوكان . It's a regional thing. These type of sentences make sense if translated word-for-word into English, however, remember that لوكان never needs conjugating.

Below are the most common kinds of conditional phrases. The way to form a phrase for an action that could possibly happen is illustrated first, then how to form a phrase for an action that is impossible.

Type I – With Past, Present, Future, and Imperative
• The Action is Possible:
This type of phrase is made up of two (or more) verbs: one in the past followed by one in the future or imperative. This construction is not the same as in English, where the first verb would be in the present tense:

إلا مشيت ل المدينة غادي نشري شي حاجة
elaa msheet l medina, ghadi neshree shee Haja
Literally: If I went to the medina I will buy something.
Meaning: If I go to the medina I will buy something.

If the second verb is in the imperative instead of the future, it takes on the meaning of ordering someone to do something:

إلا مشيتي ل المدينة شريلي شي حاجة

elaa msheetee l medina, shreelee shee Haja

Literally: If you went to the medina, buy for me something!
Meaning: If you go to the medina, buy something for me!

This type of sentence (whether with the future or imperative) can also be constructed using the irregular verbs that conjugate like nouns (such as *to have*), which requires the past tense كان:

إلا كان عندك شي مشكيل صلّي

elaa kaan 3andek shee mushkel, Sallee!

Literally: If you were you had a problem, pray!
Meaning: If you have a problem, pray!

In this last type of sentence, notice that the past tense verb كان has to agree in number and gender with the noun, which in that example was مشكيل. If the noun was feminine, the past tense verb used would be كانت.

- *The Action is Not Possible:*
This type of sentence is the most complicated sort of conditional sentence. The basic meaning is that if some condition had been met in the past, some action in the future would have occurred, but did not. It follows the form of *if I (past)(future), I would have (past)*:

لوكان عرفت بلّي غادي تمشي ل المدينة لوكان مشيت معاك

lokan aarft bllee ghradi tmshii l'medina, lokan msheet m3aaak

Literally: If I knew you will go to the medina, I would have gone with you
Meaning: If I had known that you were going to the medina, I would have gone with you

In the example above, the sentence implies that at some discrete point in the past, had I known you were going to the medina, my plans *would have been* to go with you, however, I did not know this, and therefore I did not go with you. You went to the medina alone, and I probably stayed at home eating buffalo wings.

This kind of phrase can be formed with the past continuous instead of just the regular past. This changes the meaning from, for example, *If I had worked* to *If I had been working*:

لوكان كنت كنخدم لوكان متّ

lokan kunt kankhdem, lokan mtt
If I had been working, I would have died

This particular sentence implies that had I been in the process of working, something (a meteor? Lightning? Landslide?) would have caused my death, but, since I was not working, I did not die. I know this is a weird example, but it was the first to come to mind.

Type II – With Continuing to do Something
• *The Action is Possible:*
The verb *to want* can be used in the conditional tense:

إلا بغيتي تزيد تاكول زيد، كول

eela bghreetee tzeed takool, zeed kool!
Literally: If you wanted to continue to eat, continue to eat!
Meaning: If you want to continue eating, continue to eat!

The fact that when this verb is conjugated in the past tense, it has the meaning of wanting something *now* is not important. Also notice the use of multiple verbs: *to continue* and *to eat* are both conjugated in the same way, first in the present and then in the imperative. For more information on using multiple verbs in the same sentence, refer to the section on using multiple verbs in one present-tense sentence.

▪ *The Action is Not Possible:*
The verb *to want* can be used in the same manner to imply that the action did not occur:

لوكان بغيتي تزيد تاكول، لوكان زيدت كليت

lokan bghreetee tzeed takool, lokan zeedtee kletee
Literally: If you had wanted to continue to eat, you would have continued to eat

This phrase implies that you did not want to continue eating, and therefore, you did not continue to eat. The rest of the sentence is formed in the exact same way as if the action had actually occurred, aside from the fact that إلا is replaced by لوكان.

Type III – With Adjectives
▪ *The Action is Possible:*
This sort of phrase is made up of an adjective followed by a verb in the future or imperative (like Type I). As above, translating this kind of phrase word for word will sound very strange. If the verb is in the future tense, it means that should a condition be met, an action will occur:

إلا كنت مريض، غادي نشوف شي طبيب

elaa kunt mreeD, ghraadi nshoof shee Tbeeb
Literally: If I was sick, I will see a doctor.
Meaning: If I get sick, I'll see a doctor.

If the verb is in the imperative tense, it means that should some certain condition be met, you are commanding some person to perform some action:

إلا كنتي مريض، زور شي طبيب

elaa kuntee mreeD, zoor shee Tbeeb

Literally: If you were sick, visit a doctor!

Meaning: Hey you! If you are sick, visit a doctor!

Recall that using adjectives in the past tense requires the verb كون, which must agree in gender and number with the adjective. In the examples above, it is a male speaking and someone speaking to a man, respectively.

- *The Action is not Possible:*

When the action is not possible, or it did not occur, it follows the form *If I had (past adjective), I would have (past)*. To change *if I had* into *if you had* or *if they had*, it is the second verb that is altered:

لوكان كنت مسالي، لوكان زرتك

lokan kunt msalee, lokan zortek

Literally: If I had been free, I would have visited you.

لوكان كنتي مسالي، لوكان زرتيني

lokan kuntee msalee, lokan zorteenee

Literally: If you had been free, you would have visited me.

Adjectives are treated here the same way as they were above, using the verb كون, and again, this verb must agree in gender and number with the adjective.

This kind of phrase represents something that most definitely did not occur. The first example above implies that, for some reason, I was not free at the particular time I'm referring to and, because of that, I did not go and visit you. I was probably eating buffalo wings, as previously mentioned.

The Passive Voice

The passive voice, in English, usually demands the word *by*, as in "this sentence was written *by me*." In that phrase, *sentence* is the subject, but it is not the one doing the action. For some reason it is not considered by grammarians to be 'good English' to use the passive voice. (Ha!) In Arabic, the passive voice is not discouraged. The passive voice is constructed simply by adding the letter ت to the beginning of the word. For example:

He stole	sirq	سرق
He was stolen	tsirq	تسرق
She was stolen	tsirqaat	تسرقات
They were stolen	tsirqoo	تسرقو

There are a lot of regional variations to the passive voice, so you may hear the occasional extra vowel sound stuffed in there someplace. ('He was eaten' could be *tenkel, tneklet, tklaa*, etc.) People are rarely stolen, but *he* and *she* here refer to male or female nouns:

The salad was stolen	shlada tsirqaat	الشلاضة تسرقات

This sentence translates literally to *the salad, she was stolen* which is a grammatically fine, though a little old-fashioned, way to translate it. The verb does not necessarily need to be in the past tense:

To swallow	srt	صرط
He was swallowed	tsrt	تصرط
He'll be swallowed	ghradee yetsrt	غادي يتصرط
To love	hebb	حبّ
He was loved	t'Hebb	تحبّ
He is loved	kayt'Hebb	كيتحبّ

59

The Causative Case

In English, the causative case is easy to identify: it uses the verb *to make*, as in *I made him give me the secret.* In Arabic, instead of using an extra verb, a *shedda*, the punctuation mark that denotes the doubling of a sound, is used. For example:

To be cold	bred	برد
To make cold	brred	برّد

When using *to make cold*, as in *the weather made me cold*, or *I will make the milk cold* the sound of the middle consonant is held for twice as long. It may be easier to recognize if it is thought of as appearing in two parts, that is, it sounds like "br-red." This verb is then conjugated just like any other verb, but with the addition of object pronouns:

To memorize	HefeDh	حفض
To make memorize	HeffeDh	حفّض
I am memorizing it (fem.)	kanHefDha	كنحفضها
I am memorizing it (masc.)	kanHefDoo	كنحفضو

(The above sentences differ because darija has no word for *it*!)

He is making me memorize it	kayHeffeDhalee	كيحفّضهالي
(Said by a woman)		

This is true for all tenses:

To hate	kreh	كره
To make hate	krreh	كرّه
I hated him	krehtoo	كرهتو
He made me hate him	krrehnoo	كرّهتو
or: krrehni fih		كرّهني فيه
I will hate him	ghradee nkrehoo	غادي نكرهو
He'll make me hate him	ghradee ykrrehoo	غادي نكرّهو
or: ghradee ykrrehni fih		غادي يكرّهني فيه

Verb Participles

Participles are like adjectives that are made from verbs. There are two different kinds: active and passive. Transitive verbs (verbs that require a direct object to make sense, i.e. the verb *to hold* in the sentence *I held the hammer*) have both an active and a passive participle; intransitive verbs (verbs that do not require a direct object, i.e. *to move* in *I moved*) have only passive participles.

Active participles have the meaning of *having (verb)ed*, while passive participles are translated as *having been (verb)ed*. With an active participle, the subject has completed an action; with a passive participle, some action has been completed on the subject.

Active participles are formed by adding an alif (aa sound) after the first consonant of the verb stem:

To write	kteb	كتب
Having written	kaatb / kaatba	كاتب \ كاتبة

Note that, since a participle is treated like an adjective, there is a male and female version of it, depending on the subject of the sentence:

Having written the letter, he left.
Hit huwa kaatb bratoo, khrj
حيت هو كاتب براتو، خرج
(literally: since he wrote his letter, he left)

Having written the letter, she left.
Hit heya kaatba bratha, khrjat
حيت هي كاتبة براتها خرجات
(literally: since she wrote her letter, she left)

Also, for some verbs, the active participle is the only way of expressing a current condition. For instance, *waaqf* (واقف) is the active participle of *wqf* (وقف), to stand:

I stand here (always)	kanwqf hnaa	كنوقف هنا
I am standing here (now)	waaqf hnaa	واقف هنا

Passive participles are a different kettle of fish altogether. Passive participles of intransitive verbs are the easier sort: they are formed by adding an 'm' to the beginning of the verb and then treating it as an adjective (adding an 'a' sound to the end when used with female subjects, etc).

To hid it[3]	khebbaa	خبّى
Having been hidden	mkhbbee	مخبّي
I hide it (all the time)	kankhebbi	كنخبي
I am hiding it (right now)	mkhbbee	مخبّي

The passive participles of transitive verbs are a mess to sort out. Generally, they are formed by adding an 'm' to the beginning of the word and a vowel between the last two consonants. The vowel is often, but not always, an 'oo' (و):

To write	kteb	كتب
Having been written	mktoob	مكتوب
It has been written	huwa mktoob	هو مكتوب

---

[3] This word refers to hiding an object and is sometimes pronounced/spelled خبع. To hide yourself, the reflexive كنتخبّى is used.

Irregular Verbs

To Be – كان

In most Arabic courses, the teacher will tell the class early on that there is no verb for *to be*. For instance, the sentence "I am a student" is just "I student." While the verb *to be* is not used in the present tense, however, it does exist and is used in more complicated tenses, as well as with adjectives and some nouns. It has shown up occasionally already in this book. The verb *to be* is:

To be	kaan	كان
I am	kankoon	كنكون
You are (m)	katkoon	كتكون
You are (f)	katkoonee	كتكوني
She is	katkoon	كتكون
He is	kaykoon	كيكون
We are	kankoonoo	كنكونو
You are (pl)	katkoonoo	كتكونو
They are	kaykoonoo	كيكونو

In the future, *to be* is conjugated like a normal verb (i.e. ghadee nkoon, ghadee tkoon, etc). In the past, it is slightly irregular:

I was	kunt	كنت
You were (m)	kunti	كنتي
You were (f)	kunti	كنتي
She was	kaant	كانت
He was	kaan	كان
We were	kn-naa	كنّا
You were (pl)	kuntoo	كنتو
They were	kaanoo	كانو

To be is always used in the infinitive when it is being used with a verb that takes a possessive ending (*to need, to have,* etc). in the simple past tense:

| I had a problem | kaan 3andi mushkeel | كان عندي مشكيل |
| I needed food | kaan khessnee makla | كان خصّني المكلة |

In other tenses, *to be* is conjugated in agreement with the verb that requires a possessive ending (i.e., <u>kan</u>koon and<u>i</u>, kaykoon and<u>ha</u>, etc.):

I usually have a problem
kankoon 3andi mushkeel
كنكون عندي مشكيل

I am going to have a problem
ghraadee nkoon 3andi mushkeel
غادي نكون عندي مشكيل

To be is also used to indicate finding one's self or to be in the state of. It translates sort of strangely in English, but it generally means *I am*:

I find myself in the Acima kankoon f Acima   كنكون ف أسيما
    (i.e., I am in the Acima, or I regularly go to the Acima. Acima is a Moroccan supermarket chain, and means 'capital'.)

She finds herself hungry   katkoon ji3aana   كتكون جيعانة
    (i.e., She is hungry, or, she is always hungry at this time)

To Be Present – كاين

The word *kayen* (كاين) is the participle of *kaan*. Literally, it means *having been*, but in everyday use it is translated as *there is, there is present,* or *there exists*.

Like all adjectives, there are three versions of kayen: masculine, feminine, and plural. Unlike other adjectives, however, they also each have negative forms, which follow the normal scheme for negation of verbs:

There is (m)	kayen	كاين
There is not (m)	makayensh	ماكاينش
There is (f)	kayena	كاينة
There is not (f)	makayenash	ماكايناش
There are	kayeneen	كاينين
There are not	makayeneensh	ماكاينينش

This form is used both to ask if a person is present, if a vendor has a certain product, if there's a train at a certain time, and so on. A few simple examples:

Is there any coke?

(literally: is coke present?/does coke exist?)

wash kayen koka?

واش كاين كوكا؟

Is Bob here?

(literally: does Bob exist here?/is Bob present?)

wash kayen Bob?

واش كاين بوب؟

No. He's not here

(literally: no, he doesn't exist/is not present)

la. makayensh.

لا. ماكاينش

***To Have* – عند**

One of the most frequently used verbs is *to have*. Unfortunately, it is an irregular verb; fortunately, it's a very simple sort of irregular verb. Instead of conjugating it with prefixes and suffixes like most other verbs, *to have* is conjugated by adding possessive suffixes like some sort of weird preposition:

I have	3ndee	عندي
You have (m or f)	3ndek	عندك
She has	3nd'ha	عندها
He has	3ndoo	عندو
We have	3ndna	عندنا
You (pl) have	3ndkom	عندكم
They have	3ndhom	عندهم

Although it is irregular, it's still negated the same way as other verbs, by adding the prefix ما and the suffix ش. Some examples:

Do you have any coke?
Wash 3andek shee koka?
واش عندك شي كوكا؟

I do not have a house.
ma3endeesh ddaar.
ماعنديش الدّار.

As with a number of other non-English languages saying that someone is 'lucky' literally translates as someone 'having luck (الزهر):

I am lucky (literally: I have luck)
3ndee zahar
عندي الزهر

I am not lucky (literally: I don't have luck)

ma3ndeesh zahar

ماعنديش الزهر

In English, it is sometimes said that a person has 'it'. As in, *"I don't know what 'it' is, but that guy's got 'it'."* It roughly means that a person is bold, successful, The Man, as it were. In Moroccan Arabic, there's a similar phrase, but the literal translation is a lot funnier:

He has 'it'

3ndoo jjbha

عندوالجبهة

(Literally: He has the forehead)[4]

Of course a person who is shy, a real wallflower or milquetoast, can be said not to have 'it':

He doesn't have 'it'

maa3ndoosh jjbha

ماعندوش الجبهة

(Literally: He does not have the forehead)

Ever have a day where you just don't feel like doing something? In Moroccan Arabic, this lack of drive is expressed with 'to have':

I don't feel like doing it

ma3ndeesh lgaana[5]

ماعنديش الڭانا

(literally: I don't have the will)

---

[4] First, this has never been said about me. Second, it should be noted that this phrase can be meant as an insult: as in, this person is so bold and successful, his behavior borders on the unacceptably salacious!

[5] This word means 'desire' or 'will' and is apparently of Spanish origin, as in *no tengo ganas*.

To Have Ever – عمّر

The verb عمّر means something along the lines of *to ever have done*, as in *did you ever* or *you have never*, just like the traditional college party game. Like the verb *to have*, this word is conjugated by adding an objective pronoun, and is also not technically a verb. It's more of an adverb. But, to English-speakers, it's all pretty much the same:

I ever	3mmernee	عمّرني
You (m or f) ever	3mmrek	عمّرك
She ever	3mmerha	عمّرها
He ever	3mmeroo	عمّرو
We ever	3mmerna	عمّرنا
You (pl) ever	3mmerkom	عمّركم
They ever	3mmerhom	عمّرهم

Clearly, *they ever...* makes no sense. Usually this verb is used with واش and a verb in the past tense to frame a question, as in *have you ever....* For example:

Have you ever seen Jaws?
wash 3mmrek shftee Jaws?
واش عمّرك شفتي جاوز؟

Has he ever lived in Morocco?
wash 3mmeroo skn f lmaghreb?
واش عمّرو سكن ف المغرب؟

Have you ever visited her?
wash 3emmrek zrteeha?
واش عمّرك زرتيها؟

To answer in the affirmative, عمّر is not used: one would just say *yes, I have...* with whatever verb was in the question in the past tense. To say that one has never done something, though, the prefix ما is used, without the suffix ش that is usually used in negations:

I have never visited her
ma3mmerni zrt'ha
ماعمّرني زرتها

He has never cooked a chicken
ma3mmeroo Tyyb ddjaj
ماعمّرو طيّب الدجاج

He has never lived in Ouarzazate [6]
ma3mmeroo skn f Ouarzazate
ماعمّرو سكن ف ورزازات

This is not the same word as *never*, however. That word is گاع:

I never eat meat
ga3 makanakulsh lHm
گاع ما كناكلش اللحم
or
makanakulsh lHm ga3
ماكناكلش اللحم گاع

(This second version is more emphatic, in case you really, really want to stress the point that you don't like the beefs.)

---

[6] Ouarzazate, The Door of the Desert, is a town in southern Morocco, famous as a location for the filming of many movies. The name literally means *noiselessly*, and is my favorite word in all of Moroccan Arabic because not a single letter connects to another.

To Need – خصّ

The word *need* is both a verb (I need a shower) and a noun (I have needs, too!) in English. In Arabic, the corresponding verb خصّ is irregular; it is conjugated like a noun, with possessive suffixes. For example:

I need	khSSnee	خصّني
You (m) need	khSSek	خصّك
You (f) need	khSSek	خصّك
He needs	khSSoo	خصّو
She needs	khSS'ha	خصّها
We need	khSSna	خصّنا
You (pl) need	khSSkoom	خصّكم
They need	khSS'hoom	خصّهم

Despite the fact that it is conjugated like a possessive noun, it is still negated in the same way as other verbs: adding the prefix ما and suffix ش :

I don't need	ma khSSneesh	ما خصّنيش
You(m) don't need	ma khSSeksh	ما خصّكش
You(f) don't need	ma khSSeksh	ما خصّكش
He doesn't need	ma khSSoosh	ما خصّوش
She doesn't need	ma khSShash	ما خصّها ش
We don't need	ma khSSnash	ما خصّنا ش
You(pl) don't need	ma khSSkoomsh	ما خصّكمش
They don't need	ma khSS'hoomsh	ما خصّهمش

These rules are enough to describe both an object that is needed (I need *a* bath) and an action that needs to be done (I need *to* bathe), which require only a noun and a verb, respectively. When describing an action that needs to be done, the same rules are followed as any time two verbs are in one

70

sentence (i.e., adding single-letter prefixes and (sometimes) suffixes to each verb after the first. For more information on this, see the section on using multiple verbs in one sentence in the present tense):

I need to	khSSnee n_____	ن _____ خصّني
You (m) need to	khSSek t_____ee	_____ت خصّك
He needs to	khSSoo y_____	ي _____ خصّو
She needs to	khSS'ha t_____	ت _____ خصّها
We need to	khSSna n_____oo	و _____ن خصّنا
You (pl) need to	khSSkoom t__oo	و _____ت خصّكم
They need to	khSS'hoom y__oo	و _____ي خصّهم

Of course, the _____ in the above is where the verb would go. To say that someone does not need to do something, the second verb (the x_____ verb) does not change; rather, the negative of خص is used.

I need a book	khSSnee ktab	خصني كتاب
I need to write	khSSnee nkteb	خصني نكتب
You (m) need to be happy	khSSk tfrah	خصك تفرح
You (m) need a key	khSSk saroot/lmeftaah	
		خصك الساروت/ المفتاح
You (f) need to relax	khSSk trtaahee	خصك ترتاحي
They need to be silent	khSShoom ysktoo	خصهم يسكتو

To Please – عجب

The verb *to like* is probably one of the most frequently used words in the English language. Unfortunately, in darija, there is not really an equivalent. Instead, the word *to please* is used; this makes things a little complicated, since you, the person, is no longer the subject of the sentence. The object that pleases you is the subject of the sentence. Conjugating the verb *to please*, عجب, is fairly easy:

I please	kan3jb	كنعجب
You (f) please	kat3jb	كتعجب
You (m) please	kat3jb	كتعجب
She pleases	kat3jb	كتعجب
He pleases	kay3jb	كيعجب
We please	kan3jboo	كنعجبو
You (pl) please	kat3jboo	كتعجبو
They please	kay3jboo	كيعجبو

To add a subject to the sentence, a possessive pronoun is added to the end of the conjugated verb (nee, ek, oo, etc.)

How to conjugate a noun is decided based on the gender of the thing that is doing the pleasing (that is, the thing that is liked). For example:

I like goat meat (m)	kay3jbnee l3anzee	يعجبني العنزي
I like liver (f)	kat3jbnee lkbda	كتعجبني الكبدة
I like tagines (pl)	kay3jbooni TTwajn	كيعجبوني الطواجن
He likes goat meat	kay3jboo l3anzee	كيعجبو العنزي
She likes liver	kat3jbha lkbda	كتعجبها الكبدة
They like tagines	kay3jbuhum TTwajn	كيعجبوهم الطواجن

Note that these sentences literally mean *it pleases me the liver*, etc., but are translated as *I like liver* and so on.

72

This verb can easily be translated in the past tense to mean *I liked something* as it is a regular verb. However, it must be remembered that even in the past, the subject of the sentence is the thing that is doing the pleasing. For example:

I liked goat meat (m)	3jbnee l3anzee	عجبني العنزي
I liked liver (f)	3jbaatnee lkbda	عجباتني الكبدة
I liked tagines (pl)	3jbnee TTwajn	عجبوني الطواجن

This is, of course, how to say that one likes an object. If one likes to do something, the verb is conjugated just the same way that the second verb in any sentence is conjugated:

I like to eat	kay3jbnee nakul	كيعجبني ناكل
She likes to travel	kay3jbha tsafr	كيعجبها تسافر
They like to learn	kay3jboo yt3allem	كيعجبو يتعلم

To Remain – بقى

The verb بقى is a Type-I irregular verb that means *to continue*, *to remain*, or *to keep on* doing something. When followed by the present tense of a verb, it means that someone is continuing to do something. بقى itself can be in the past, present, or future tenses, and is the sort of Type-I Irregular verb where ى changes to ي before addition of the past-tense suffixes. For example:

I kept on working   bqeet kankhdem   بقيت كنخدم
(Literally: I remained working)

I'm continuing to work kanqba kankhdem كنبقى كنخدم
(Literally: I am remaining I am working)

I will continue to work
ghradee nbqa kankhdem   غادي نبقى كنخدم
or:
ghradee nbqa nkhedem   غادي نبقى نخدم

When negated, بقى literally means *to not remain* but is more easily translated as *not anymore* or *no longer*:

I am no longer working (or: I don't work anymore)
mabqeetsh kankhdem
مابقيتش كنخدم

Finally, the active participle of *to remain* is باقي. This word is used more frequently than the verb form and can be translated as "still" (although it literally translates as *having remained*):

I still work   baqee kankhdem   باقي كنخدم

To Want – بغى

The verb بغى has two meanings in darija. When conjugated in the past tense it means *to want* in the present; the meaning is that, up until this point, someone wanted something, and they currently still want it. When conjugated in the present tense, it means *to like*.

بغى is a Type I irregular verb. To conjugate it in the past tense, the final ى becomes an ي in the first- and second-person forms and then the past tense suffixes are added:

I want	bghreet	بغيت
You (m or f) want	bghreetee	بغيتي
He wants	bghra	بغى
She wants	bghrat	بغات
We want	bghreena	بغينا
You (pl) want	bghreetoo	بغيتو
They want	bghraw	بغاو

Remember that while this literally translates as *I wanted, you wanted,* etc., the meaning is in the present tense: *I want, you want*, and so on. This word can be followed by either a noun (wanting something) or a verb (wanting to do something). For example:

I want some mint
bghreet na3na3
بغيت النعناع
Literally: I wanted some mint

He wants to sing
bghraa yghrennee
بغى يغنّي
Literally: He wanted to sing

As before, when saying that someone wants to do something (i.e. following بغى with a verb) the second verb is treated the same way as the second verb in any sentence.

To express wanting to do something in the past, the verb كان (kaan) must be used. This verb is often used to express the more complicated tenses (i.e. the past progressive, etc.) so it is no surprise that it appears here.

He wanted to sing
kaan bghraa yghrennee
كان بغى يغنّي
Literally: He was he wanted to sing

When conjugated in the present tense, the ى at the end of بغى becomes an ي in every form; then the present-tense prefixes (and, for plurals, suffixes) are added:

I like	kanbghree	كنبغي
You (m or f) like	katbghree	كتبغي
She likes	katbghree	كتبغي
He likes	kaybghree	كيبغي
We like	kanbghreew	كنبغيو
You (pl) like	katbghreew	كتبغيو
They like	kaybghreew	كيبغيو

Because بغى is a Type I Irregular verb, here the masculine- and feminine-singular forms are identical. Again, either nouns or verbs can follow بغى in the present tense:

I like soda (or pop, or coke, or however you say it)
kanbhree lemonada
كنبغي المونادا

76

They like to argue
kaybghreew ytkhaaSSmoo
كيبغيو يتخاصمو

When used with an object pronoun, بغى means *to like* in the same way schoolyard children talk about who 'likes' who (that is, it can be translate as *to love*). There is another verb for *to love* that can be used to avoid confusion:

I like (or love) you	kanbghreek	كنبغيك
I love you	kan'Hebbek	كنحبّك

The first example leaves room for speculation as to whether I love or just like a person; the second one makes it completely clear. Just to make things confusing, the first one is preferred in the north of the country. Look: if you love someone, you should have no trouble expressing it to them regardless of which word you choose. In fact, go buy that special someone some flowers. They deserve it.

Questions Words

(Yes or no?)   waash   واش

This is used when asking a question that demands a yes/no answer, like "do you have any gum?" or "is this the bus to Tangier?" or "is that donkey following us?"

Who	shkoon	شكون
When	foqash/foyakh/eemta	فوقاش / فوياخ /إمتى
Where	feen / faayen	فين / فاين
Why	3llash	علاش
How	kifash	كيفاش
What	shnoo / shnee / ash	أش / شنّي/ شنو
Which	ash mn / shmn	أشمن/ شمن

Note that when using comparative adjectives as in "which pizza topping is better?" the word *ama* (أما) is used to mean "which" instead of أشمن . Also, for the examples above, the second choices (foyakkh, faayen, etc. are more likely to be found in the north of the country).

From where	mneen	منين
With whom	m3a mn	مع من
Whose	dial mn	ديال من
With what	baash	باش
In what	faash	فاش
Of what	dial ash	ديال اش
Really?!	bSSah bSSah	ب الصّحّ ب الصّحّ
How much	bsh'Haal	بشحال

This context generally refers to prices, as in "how much do I owe?" and serves as good segue to begin talking about money.

Talking about Money

شحال has two meanings: "how much?" and "how many?" depending on what kind of noun it refers to. If it followed by a non-quantifiable object (like "money") it means "how much" and if it is followed by a quantifiable noun (like "dirhams") it means "how many." For example:

How much money?	sh'Haal d floos?	شحال د الفلوس ؟
How many dirhams?	sh'Haal d draahm?	شحال د الدراهم ؟
How many dirham?	sh'Haal mn dirham	شحال من درهم

The preposition د is used with the singular form of a non-quantifiable noun (money) and the plural form of a quantifiable noun (dirhams). Min (من) is used with the single form of a quantifiable noun (dirham) and has the same meaning as the one above it, except that it sounds a little old fashioned.

Morocco's monetary system is based on the Moroccan Dirham (DH or MAD). Dirham are available in 200, 100, 50, and 20 DH bills (blue, beige, green, and purple, respectively). 10 DH coins are gold around the outside and silver in the center; 5 DH coins are the other way around. There are also 2 and 1 DH coins.

There are two other common units of measurement: ryals (20 ryals per dirham) and centimes (also called franks; 100 centimes per dirham). Brass-colored 10, 20, and 50 centime coins are frequently used (or, ½, 1, and 2½ ryal coins, if you prefer to think of it that way).

Ryals and centimes are only rarely used, but some old-timers like to price things in ryals, especially outside of the cities. There are also different kinds of ryals: a Casablanca ryal isn't the same as a Tangier ryal. They also use Francs up north. I was never able to properly understand prices in ryals or francs. I don't know why, but I just couldn't get it.

Telling Time

To tell time, three words are used: the pronoun هادي, a number, and a modifier (i.e., if it is exactly a certain time, half past, or whatever). This is all the grammar that is needed.

As in America, Moroccans use a 12-hour system. The definite article is used (i.e. *the one* as opposed to *one*), which means that for the numbers 1, 5, 10, and 11, the ل sound is pronounced, and for the other numbers, the first consonant is pronounced for twice as long:

One	lwaHda	الوحدة
Two	jjooj	الجّوج
Three	ttlata	التلاتة
Four	rerb3a / llarb3a	اللّربعة / الرّبعة
Five	lkhamsa	الخمسة
Six	sssta	السّتّة
Seven	ssb3a	السّبعة
Eight	tmenya	التّمنية
Nine	ts3ood	التّسعود
Ten	l3ashra	العشرة
Eleven	lhdaash	الحضاش
Twelve	ttnaash	الطّناش

These numbers are used for the hours. The modifiers are:

10 minutes	qsmaayn	قسمين / قسميان
Quarter after	rba3	ربع
20 minutes	tooloot	تلت
Half	nuss	نصّ
Quarter till	lla rub	لّا رب
Before	qall / gheer	قلّ/غير
At the same time	f nfs lwqt	ف نفس الوقت

Exactly	nishan/waqfa/qddqdd	نيشان / واقفة/ قدّقدّ

(Waqfa is preferred in the north; qddqdd in Fes)

Using 9:00 as an example, one would tell the time by saying:

9:00	ts300d nishan	التسعود نيشان
9:05	ts300d oo qsm	التسعود قسم
9:10	ts300d oo qsmaayn	التسعود و قسمين
9:15	ts300d oo rba3	التسعود و ربع
9:20	ts300d oo tuloot	التسعود و تلت
9:25	ts300d oo khamsa oo 3ushrin	التسعود و خمسة وعشرين
In fes:	ts300d oo khamsa qsaam	التسعود و خمسة قسام
9:30	ts300d oo nss	التسعود و نصّ
9:35	ts300d oo sb3 qsaam	التسعود و سبع قسام
9:40	ts300d qll tuloot	التسعود قل تلت
9:45	ts300d lla roob	التسعود لا رب
9:50	ts300d qll qsmayn	التسعود قل قسمين
9:55	ts300d qll qsm	التسعود قل قسم

Conjunctions

Conjunctions are the little words used in complicated sentences. There are no particular grammatical rules to remember here; instead, the words simply have to be memorized. The good news is that if even a small number of these words can be remembered, more and more complex sentences can be constructed.

Who, whom, which, and *that* are all the same word:
The woman who I love is pretty
lmraa llee kan'Hebb zweena / mziwna
لمرا اللّي كنحبّ زوينة/ مزيونة

The chicken that I am eating is very big [7]
djaj llee kanakool wafee bzzaaf
الدَّجاج اللّي كناكل واقي بزّاف

Similarly, *since, when,* and *because* are interchangeable in a lot of ways. Sentences using this word can usually be translated in three different ways, but express the same idea:

Since I was in the city, I saw her
Heet kunt f lmedina, shft'ha
حيت كنت ف المدينة، شقتها

When I was in the city, I saw her
melli kunt f lmdina shft'ha.
مللي كنت فالمدينة شفتها

Because I was in the city I saw her
3llahaqqash kunt f lmdina shft'ha.
علاحقاش كنت فالمدينة شقتها

---

[7] 'Wafee' is used for 'large', because using 'kbeer' for 'big' might make people interpret the sentence to mean "the chicken that I am eating is very *old*."

When using the phrase "before," the verb is in the present tense, but without the prefix *ka*:

I usually sing before eating
ghraleban kanghranee qbl ma nakul
غالبان كنغنّي قبل ما ناكل

When using the phrase "after," both verbs must be in the same tense:
I always eat after I sing
deema kanakool mn b3d ma kanghrennee
ديما كناكول من بعد ما كنغنّي

"As long as" is followed by a verb and then, usually, the future tense:

As long as I am living here, I will eat couscous
mahaddi kanskun hna, ghradee nakool seksoo / kesksu
ماحدّي كنسكن هنا، غادي ناكل الكسكسو، سكسو

The phrase listed here as meaning *without* is used only with verbs. To use it with nouns, the second word is dropped:

I slept without dreaming of you
n3ast bla ma n'Hlm beek
نعست بلا ما نحلم بيك

I want a pizza without cheese
bghreet shee pizza bla fromaj [8]
بغيت شي بيتزة بلا فروماج

---

[8] 'jben' (جبن) may be used instead of 'fromaj', similar to 'soda' vs. 'pop'. 'Jben' is of Moroccan origin, and 'fromaj' is just a French word that's become widely used in Morocco.

Baash (باش) means "in order to." For example:

I went to the medina in order to buy something
msheet lmedina baash nshree shee haja
مشيت ل المدينة باش نشري شي حاجة

It is also used with some adjectives; for example mujood (مجود) means "ready." In Arabic, it is usually paired with "in order to", which combine to mean "to be ready":

I am ready to...   ana mujood baash...   ...أنا مجود باش
            (Literally: I am ready in order to...)

Are you ready to...   waash nta mujood baash... ...واش نت باش
            (Literally: Are you ready in order to...)

We are not ready to...
hnaa mamjoodeensh baash...
حنا مامجودينش باش...

We are not ready to...
hnaa mashi mujoodin baash
حنا ماشي مجودين باش

باش is also used with the word wjjd (وجّد), which means "to prepare."

Prepare to eat!
Wjjd raasek baash tkool!
وجّد راسك باش تكول
(Literally: Prepare your head in order to you eat!)

Many other conjunctions are used in pretty much the same way as they are used in English:

From now on, I will speak only Arabic
mn daba foq, ghradee ntkellem ghrir b l3arabiyya
من دابا لفوق، غادي نتكلّم غير ب العربية

I study in order to speak well
kanqraa bash ntkellem meziaan
كنقرى باش نتكلّم مزيان

I drank a lot, then I vomited
shrebt bzzaf, 3ad reddit 9
شربت بزّاف، عاد ردّيت

Wherever there is money, there are problems
feen ma kanu lfloos, kayneen lmashaakel
فين ما كانو الفلوس، كاينين المشاكل

Although I'm American, I try to speak Arabic
wah-ha ana merikanee, kan'Hawl ntkellem b l3arabeyya
وخّا انا مريكاني، كنحاول نتكلّم ب العربية

Whenever I am in the city, I visit her
wqt ma kankoon f lmedina, kanzoorha
وقت ما كنكون ف المدينة، كنزورها

---

9 For 'to vomit' one can use rdd (رَدّ), tqeeya (تقيّى), or gllt (گلّت). I hope that this information is of no use to you.

Prepositions

In any language, prepositions are an unpleasant thing to have to learn. They're small and tricky. Prepositions can mean different things when they are used with different verbs, and in Arabic they are sometimes used with words that do not require prepositions in English (for instance, *to defend* in Arabic translates literally as *to defend about*).

Below are the most common prepositions in Arabic. How the preposition is used with a pronoun ending (i.e. *for him, about her, to us,* etc.) is given first, and then the verbs that require that preposition are listed. For most of these verbs a preposition is obligatory; for some of it's just used more often than not.

Sometimes the meaning of a verb changes based on which preposition is used. For instance, the verb 'daaz' means *to go through* or *to go past*, depending on if it is used with *min* or *3la*. The verb 3ayT means to *call*, if used with l or 3la, or *to telephone*:

To call	3ayT l	عيّط ل
"	3ayT 3la	عيّط على
To telephone	3ayT b	عيّط ب
To telephone	3ayT	عيّط

Miscellaneous Prepositions

Some prepositions can go with any verb, so long as the sentence makes sense. Here are some of them.

aboard	f	ف
Above	fuq	فوق
Across from	qbaalt	قبالة
after/following	b3d	بعد
among	wust	وسط
around (time)	jooayeh	جوايه
around (the corner)	Doora	ضورة
As	men lee	من لي
Before	qbl	قبل
behind	moora	مورا
Below/under/down	tht	تحت
Beside	zheneb	جنب
between	bin	بين
beyond	lihin men	ليهن من
But	walakeen	ولكن
during	f waqt	ف الوقت
except	maa3daa	ماعدا
excepting	men ghreer	من غير
Facing	mqaabl m3	مقابل مع
in front of/past	qddam	قدّام
Into	b	ب
Like	bhal	بحال
Near	qreeb	قريب
next to	Hdaa	حدا
Of	d	د

off/from	min	من
opposite	3ks	عكس
Outside	berra	برا
Over	fuq men	فوق من
regarding	amma	أمَّا
Than	min	من
through	f	ف
Toward	m3a	مع
Until	htta L	حتَّى ل
Within	dakhel	داخل
Without	bla	بلا

ل – *To, For*

The preposition ل almost always translates as *to* or *for*. For some verbs, this preposition is obligatory, but it can also be used with any verb that is being done *to* or *for* someone (i.e. *I cooked this for him*). With the pronoun endings:

To me	leeya / lili	ليّا ليلي
To you	lik / lilek	لك ليلك
To him	leh / loo / liloo	ليه \ لو \ ليلو
To her	leeha / lila	ليها ليلا
To us	leena / lilna	لينا ليلنا
To you (pl)	leekom	ليكم
To them	leehom	ليلهم

Which pronoun ending you use will vary depending upon what city you live in.

Verbs that frequently use, or require, l:

To be possible for	yemkin l	يمكن ل
To bring to	jaab l	جاب ل
To explain to	fssr l	فسّر ل
To forgive, permit	smeH l	سمح ل
To pay back	rdd l	ردّ ل
To say to	gaal l	گال ل
To say to (northern)	qaal l	قال ل
To send to	sift l	صيفط ل
To wave at	sheeyyer l	شيّر ل

Bring him/ it to me!	jeeboo lee!	جيبو لي
I will pay you back	ghradee nrdd lik	غادي نردّ لك
Pardon me	smeH lee	سمح لي

ف – *In*

The preposition ف usually means *in*, but occasionally means *about, on,* or *at*. With the pronoun endings:

For me	feeyya	فيّا
For you	feek	فيك
For him	feeh	فيه
For her	feeha	فيها
For us	feena	فينا
For you (pl)	feekom	فيكم
For them	feehom	فيهم

When used with pronouns, f can take on the meaning of 'I have' and when used with an adjective, the meaning of 'I am':

| I have the flu | feeyya rwah | فيّا رّواح |
| I am cold | feeyya bared | فيّا بارد |

Verbs that frequently use, or require, f:

To wonder at	khammem f	خمّم ف
To attend	HDar f	حضر ف
To ask about	soowwel f / 3la	سوّل ف/على
To take care of / look after	t'halla f	تهلا ف
To cause to	tsbbeb f	تسبّب ف
To continue in (classes, etc.)	stamr f	ستمرّ ف
To control	T'Hakkem f	تحكّم ف
To glare at / give the stink eye	khanzr f	خنزر ف
To gossip about	hDr f	هضر ف
To neglect	smeh f	سمح ف
To participate in	shaark f	شارك ف
To pass (a test, etc.) / succeed	njaH f	نجح ف
To think about	fkkar f	فكّر ف
To trust	taaq f	تاق ف

I trusted (in) him	tqt feeh	تقت قيه
We gossip about her	kanhDroo feeha	كنهضرو فيها
I think about him/it a lot	kanfkkar feeh bizzaf	كنفكّر فيه بزّاف

ب – *With*

ب means *with*, but usually only when referring to non-human items. For instance, it would be used for *pizza with anchovies* but not *dinner with Anthony*. It would also be used in *with the help of Eric...* because it modifies *help* and not *Eric*. It not infrequently also translates as *by, by means of, in, of, about,* or *from*. With the pronoun endings:

With me	beeyya	بيّا
With you	beek	بيك
With him	beeh	بيه
With her	beeha	بيها
With us	beena	بينا
With you (pl)	beekom	بيكم
With them	beehom	بيهم

Verbs that frequently use, or require, b:

To acknowledge	3tarf b	عترف ب
To believe in	aamn b	أمن ب
To celebrate/party	htafl b	حتافل ب
To be in/take charge of	tkllef b	تكلّف ب
To be concerned about	htemm b	هتمّ ب
To contact	ttaSSalb	تّصل ب
To dream about	Hlem b	حلم ب
To flatter (a woman only)	tghrazzl b	تغزّل ب
To marry with	tzewwj b	تزوّج ب
Not to regret (separation from)	skhaa b	سخى ب
To be very (lit: die of)	maat b	مات ب
To welcome	raH-Heb b	رحّب ب

I am married to her
(Ana) mzewwej beeha
(أنا) مزوّج بيها

We dream of peace
kanHlemnoo b salaam
كنحلمو ب السلام

I am dying of hunger
kanmoot bjoo3
كنموت بالجوع
(Not literally; it means "I'm very hungry")

I didn't regret separating from you
(Figuratively: I don't miss you)
skheet beek
سخيت بيك
(Note: this is not true. I miss you, baby.)

على – *On, About*

This preposition generally translates as *on* or *about*. Sometimes it translates as *against, to,* or *at*. Some words in English that do not require a preposition (such as *to defend*) use this preposition; in that sense it is also untranslatable. With the pronoun endings:

On me	3leeya	عليّا
On you	3leek	عليك
On him	3leeh	عليه
On her	3leeha	عليها
On us	3leena	علينا
On you (pl)	3leekom	عليكم
On them	3leehom	عليهم

Verbs that frequently use, or require, 3la:

To catch up to	khlT 3la	خلط على
"	lHeq 3la	لحق على
To complain to	tshkka 3la	تشكّى على
To be content with	rDa 3la	رضى على
To defend	daf3 3la	دافع على
To die for (or love, be crazy for, etc.)	maat 3la	مات على
To lie to	kdb 3la	كذب على
To make fun of	dHk 3la	ضحك على
"	tflla 3la	تفلّى على
To go by	daaz 3la	داز على
To govern/judge	Hkm 3la	حكم على
To say hello to, shake hands with	sellem 3la	سلّم على

To ignore[10]	miyyek 3la	ميّك على
To invite	3rD 3la	عرض على
To feel jealous about	ghaar 3la	غار على
To keep	haaDd 3la	حافظ على
To lean	tekka 3la	تكّى على
	qalleb 3la	قلّب على
To look for	fettesh 3la	فتّش على
To maintain	haafdD3la	حاقظ على
To make difficult for, maltreat someone	tkrfs 3la	تكرفس على
To miss (i.e. not make in time)	mshaa 3la	مشى على
To oblige	frD 3la	فرض على
"	bezzez 3la	بزّز على
To overcome	tghrelleb 3la	تغلّب على
To push (a button)	werrek 3la	ورّك على
"	brk 3la	برك على
To rely on	3awwel 3la	عوّل على
To remember	3ql 3la	عقل على

I missed the train
mshaa 3liyya traan
مشى عليّا التران

I love him to death
kanmoot 3leeh
كنموت عليه
(Literally: I am dying about him.)

---

10 Slang, derived from the word for plastic shopping bag. More or less means 'to pay as much attention to as one would to a plastic bag.'

مع – *With*

مع is used with people (i.e. in *dinner with Anthony* but not *pizza with onion*). Sometimes it means *against* or *along*.

With me	m3aya	معايا
With you	m3ak	معك
With him	m3ah	معه
With her	m3aha	معها
With us	m3ana	معنا
With you (pl)	m3akom	معكم
With them	m3ahom	معهم

Verbs that frequently use, or require, m3a:

To become known to	t3arf m3a	تعارف مع
To agree with	ttafq m3a	تّفق مع
To argue with	tkhaasm m3a	تخاصم مع
To become friends with	tSaHb m3a	تصاحب مع
To consult with	tshawer m3a	تشاور مع
To cooperate with	t3aawn m3a	تعاون مع
To deal/treat with	t3aamil m3a	تعامل مع
To differ from	khtalf 3la	ختلف مع
To exchange with	tbaadl m3a	تبادل مع
To face	tqaabl m3a	تقابل مع
To laugh with	DHk m3a	ضحك مع
To meet with	tlaaqaa m3a	تلاقى مع
To stay with	bqaa m3a	بقى مع
To sympathize with	t3aaTf m3a	تعاطف مع

I dealt with it	t3aamilt m3ah	تعاملت معه
We agree with her	kanttafqna m3aha	كنتّفق معها
He faced them	tqaabl m3ahom	تقابل معهم
Around ten o'clock	m3a l'ashra	معا العشرة

96

من – *From*

This preposition generally does not take pronoun endings and translates as *from*, in the sense of *I am from Morocco*. Some verbs that frequently use, or require, min:

To be afraid of	khaaf min	خاف من
To benefit from	stafd min	ستفد من
To complain about	tshkka min	تشكَّى من
To move away from, distance oneself from	ba33d min	بعَد من
To exterminate (archaic)	tkhalleS min	تخلَّص من
To get rid of	tkhalleS min	تخلَّص من
"	t'hnna min	تهنَّى من
To get/go through	daaz min	داز من
To request	Tleb min	طلب من
To turn down the volume	nqeS min	نقص من
To let go of	Tleq min	طلق من

Does he complain about her?
waash kaytshkka menha
واش كيتشكَّى منها

I benefited from it
stafdt menoo
ستفدت منو

97

Appendix I (a) – Food

For words with two translations listed, the second one (i.e. lower) is generally more frequent toward the north of the country. Northern words for food, when different, are often from Spanish. Finally, words with two transliterations and one spelling are just pronounced differently depending on region.

Vegetables	khdra	خضرة
Artichokes	lqoq	لقوق
	lgoob	لݣوب
Beets	lbarba	الباربا
Cabbage	lmkower	المكوّر
	lkrunb	الكرونب
Carrots	kheezo	خيزو
	ja3da	الجعدة
Cauliflower	sheefloor	الشفلور
	kulifloor	كليفلوور
Celery	kraafs	الكرافص
Cucumber	khyaar	الخيار
Eggplant	dnjaal	الدنجال
	dbenjal	الدبنجال
Garbanzo beans	Hmmss/Hummis	الحمص
Gourd	slaoui	السلاوي
	qra3 slaoui	القرع السلاوية
Green Bean	larikoo	الاريكو
	loobiya	اللوبية
Green peas	jelbaana	الجّلبانة
Leek	bwaaroo	البوارو
Lentils	l3ds	العدس
Lettuce	lkhass	الخس
Noodles	sh-sh3reeya	الشعريا
Okra	mlookheeyya	الملوخية

Olives	zeetoon	الزيتون
Onion	b'SSla	البصلة
Pepper	l'felfla	الفلفلة
Potatoe	baTaTa	البطاطا
Pumpkin	gr3a	الكَرعة
	qra3	القرع
Radishes	fjl	الفجل
Rice	rooz	الروز
Salad [11]	shlaada	الشلاضة
Soy beans	loobeeya	اللوبية
Tomatoe	matisha	مطيشة
Turnips	left	اللفت
Zucchini	korjeet	الكورجيط
	q'ra3	القرع

Spices

Basil	Hbeq	الحبق
Black pepper	lebzaar	البزار
Cinnamon	qrfa	القرفة
Cloves	qrnful	القرنفل
Coriander	qssboor	القصبور
Cumin	camoon	الكامون
	caymoon	الكيمون
Flour	dgeeg	الدگيگ
	T'Heen	الطحين
Garlic	tooma	التومة
	tawm	التوم
Ginger	skinjbeer	سكينجبير
Honey	3sel	العسل
Hot pepper	l'Harr	الحار

---

[11] In slang, the word 'salad' means 'mess.' As in, "Ugh, who made this salad?! There's junk everywhere!"

Mint	na3na3	النعناع
Nutmeg	gooza	الگَوزة
Oregano	z3tr	الزعتر
Paprika	t'Hmira	التحميرة
Parsley	m3dnoos	المعدنوس
Saffron	z3fraan	الزعفران
Salt	melha	الملحة
Sesame seeds	jjaljlan	الجَاجلان
Chili powder	soudaniya	السودانية
Sugar	sokaar	السكر
Tumeric	khrqoom	الخرقوم
Verbena	lweeza	اللويزة
Winter Mint	sheeba	الشيبة
Fruit	fakeeya	فاكية
	fruta (Spanish)	فروتة
Apple	tffaH	التفاح
Apricot	mshmaash	المشماش
Avocado	laavokaa	لاڤوكا
Banana	banan	البنان
Berries	toot	التوت
Cherry	hbb lmlook	حب الملوك
Dates	tmar	التمر
Figs	kermoos	الكرموس
Grape	3nb/ 3ineb	العنب
Honeydew Melon	sweehla	سويهلة
Kiwi	keewee	الكيوي
Lemon	HameD	الحامض
	lemon	اللمون
Mushroom	fuggi3	الفگّيع
Nectarine	shahdeeyya	الشهدية
Orange	lemon (southern)	الليمون

100

English	Transliteration	Arabic
Orange	l'tsheen (northern)	اللتشين
Peach	khoukh	الخوخ
Pear	lingaas	اللَّكَّاص
	bo3weed	البعويد
Pineapple	lananas	اناناس
Plum	berqoq	البرقوق
Pomegranate	rumman	الرمان
Raisins	zzbeeb	الزبيب
Strawberry	frez	الفريز
	fresa	الفرسة
Tangerine	mandarin	مندرين
Watermelon	dellah	الدلاح
Meat	lHam	اللحم
Beef	begree	البكَري
Bone	3Dm	العضم
Chicken	djaj	الدجاج
	jjdad	الجَداد
Fat	sh'Hma	الشحمة
Fish	Hoat	الحوت
Goat	m3zee	المعزي
	3nzee	العنزي
Ground Meat	kefta	الكفتة
Heart	qelb	القلب
Lamb	ghrenmee	الغنمي
Liver	kebda	الكبدة
Lungs	riyya	الريا
Rabbit	qneeya	قنية
	qlayna	قلاينة
Sardine	sardeen	السردين
Sausage	ssauseet	الصوسيط
	salchichat	سالشيشات

Shrimp	qimroon	القيمرون
	gamba (Spanish)	الكّمبا
Sole	Sool	السّول
	linguado	لنگواضو
Spleen	TiHaan	الطيحان
Snail	baboosh	بابوش
Tuna	Toon	الطون
Turkey	beebee	بيبي
Whiting	mirla	الميرلة
	peshkadia	بشكادية

Fluids

Coffee	qahwa	قهوة
Honey	3sel	عسل
Jam	konfiteer	كونفيتير
Juice / Milkshake	3aSeer	عصير
Milk	Hleeb	حليب
Mint tea	atay b na3na3	أتاي ب النعناع
Oil	zeet	الزيت
Soda pop	limonada	المونادا
Soup	H'reera	حريرة
Tea	atay	أتاي
Vinegar	khell	خلّ
Water	lma	الما

Nuts

Peanuts	kawkaw	كاوكاو
	biyan	بيّان
Almonds	looz	اللوز
	llawz	النّوى
	nnwa	نّوا
Walnuts	grgaa3	الگرگّاع

Staples

Baguette	komeera [12]	كميرة
Bread	khobz	خبز
Butter	zubda	زبدة
Cake (in general)	Halwa	حلوة
	pasta	بستا
Candy [13]	faneeda	فنيدة
Candy [14]	Halwa d lgomaa	حلوة د لكّومة
Cheese	fromage	فروماج
Egg	bayDa	بيضة
Rice	rooz/rawz	روز

Adjectives

Bland/Unsalted	msoos / a / een	مسوس / ة / ين
Boiled	mslooq / a / een	مسلوق / ة / ين
Burnt	mhrooq / a / een	محروق / ة / ين
Cold	bared / a / een	بارد / ة / ين
Cooked	Tayeb / a / een	طايب / ة / ين
Delicious	ldeed /a /een	لديد / ة / ين
Delicious	bneen /a / een	بنينة / ة /ين
Fresh	tri / yaa /yeen	طري / ة / ين
Fried	mqlee / yya / een	مقلي / ة / ين
Full	shb3aan / a / een	شبعان / ة / ين
Grilled	Meshoui / a / een	مشوي / ة / ين
Hot	skhoon / a / skhaan	سخون / ة / سخان
Hungry	ji3aan / a /een	جيعان / ة / ين
Overcooked	fayet qyas	فايت القياس
Roasted	m'Hammar	محمّر
Salty	malH / a / een	مالح / ة / ين

---

[12] From the Spanish 'comer,' meaning 'to eat'.
[13] The kind that comes in foil wrappers.
[14] The squishy kind, like gummy bears.

Spicy	harr / a / een	حارّ / ة / ين
Steamed	mfewwer / a / een	مفوَّر / ة / ين
	mbakhkhar/mbakh-khra/een	مبخر / ة/ ين
Sweet	Hlou / a / een	حلو / ة / ين
Thirsty	3etshaan / a /een	عطشان / ة / ين
Vegetarian	Nabatee-yya-yeen	نباتية

Appendix I (b) – At the Doctor's Office

There are four ways for you to say that you are ill. To fill in the blanks, use the names of body parts or types of illnesses.

I am sick in my _	ana mreeD b ___	_ ب انا مريض ب
I have ___	3andee ___	___ عندي
I feel in my ___	kanHss b ___	___ كنحسّ ب
I have (lit.: in me)_	feyya ___	___ فيّ
My ___ hurts	kayDrrnee ___	___ كيضرّني
What hurts you?	shnoo kayDrrek?	شنّو كيضرّك ؟

(Note that the كي prefix is used, because the questioner doesn't know the gender of what is hurting you)

What do you have?   shnoo 3andek?   شنّو عندك؟
(i.e. what's wrong with you?)

Does something hurt you?
waash katDrrek shee haja?
واش كتضرّك شي حاجة ؟

Did you take any medicine?
waash sta3meltee shee dwa?
واش ستعملتي شي دوا؟
(Literally: Did you use any medicine?)

With what?   baash?   باش ؟
(i.e., what is wrong with you?)

Hey, are you okay?

(To a man)	(To a woman)
maalek yak labaas[15]?	maalki yakee labaas?
مالك ياك لاباس ؟	مالكي ياكي لاباس ؟

---

[15] In the north (Tangier, Tetuan, etc.) This form is used for both genders.

Hey, are you okay? (To people)
malekom yak labaas?
مالكم ياك لاباس ؟
(Note that to address different people, only the
termination of the first word changes)

I will give you some medicine
ghradee n3Teek shee dwa
غادي نعطيك شي دوا

I will write you some medicine
ghradee nkteb lk shee dwa
غادي نكتب لك شي دوا
(i.e., I will give you a prescription)

I have an allergy to...
3andee Hsaaseyya d...
عندي الحساسيّة د ...

Cotton balls	qtn	القطن
Cream	dehnaa	الدهنة
	crema	الكريمة
Cream	pomaada	پ/بومادة
Drops	tqteera /quTra	تقطيرة/ قطرة
Laxative	musahhil	مسهّل
Needle /s	lyebra / libaaree/ shooka	ليبرة / ليباري/ شوكة
	keena /aat	كينة / ات
Pill /s	pastiyya /aat	پسطيّا
Pill /s	faneeda / faaneed	فنيدة / فانيد
Shot /s	sh-shooka	شوكة
	shwaaki	شواكي
Soap	Sabun	الصابون
Stitch	ghorza	غرزة

Syrup	seeroo	سيرو
	kharabi	خرابي
A cold	rrwah	الرّواح
Allergies	Hasaasiyya	الحساسية
Asthma	Deeqaa	الضيقة
Blood	demm	الدمّ
Cancer	saraTaan	سرطان
Constipation	imsaak	إمساك
Cough	lkeHHa	الكحّة
	ssu3la	السّعلة
Coughing	lkeHHa	الكحة
Diabetic	sukkar	السكر
Diarrhoea	ishaal	إسهال
Dizziness	dokha	دوخة
Fever	skhaana	السخانة
Hernia	fetq	فتق
Hoarseness	behha	بحة
Indigestion	3usr lhaDm	عسر الهضم
Injury	jurH	جرح
Itching (scabies)	Hekka	حكة
Lump	kutla	كتلة
Pregnant	Hamla/ Hubla/	حاملة/حبلى
	3ayyana	عيانة
	muhoola	موحولة
Smallpox	jedree	جدري
Suffering	3daab	العداب
Tiredness (or pregnancy!)	le3ya	العيا
Typhus	ttifus	التيفوس
To hurt/ burn	hraq	حرق
To immunize	jleb	جلب

English	Transliteration	Arabic
To immunize	leqqaH	لقّاح
To fake illness	tuboohT	تبوحط
To make sick	marred	مرّض
To protect	HaafeD	حافظ
To put on cream	d'hen	دهن
To scratch / rub	hakk	حكّ
To sneeze	3Tes	عطس
To take care of	qaabl	قابل
To vomit	tqayya	تقيّى
Ambulance	bulancia amboolans	بلانسيا آمبولانس
Appointment	randivoo maw3id mee3Aad	رانديفو موعد ميعاد
Dentist	Tbeeb dial snaan	طبيب ديال السنان
Diet	reejeem	ريجيم
Doctor (all parts)	Tbeeb	طبيب
Doctor (children)	Tbeeb khtiSaSee f draaree- l3yaal	طبيب ختصاصي ف الدراري
Doctor (head and stomach)	tbeeb khtiSaSee	طبيب ختصاصي
Hospital	sbeetar	السبيطار
Laboratory	mokhtabar	مختبر
Nurse	fermlia	الفرمليّة
Operation	3amaliyya	عملية
Pharmacy	ffrmseean- farmacia	الفرمسيان
Test	teHleel	تحليل
Vaccination	telqeeH	تلقيح

Appendix I (c) – Body Parts

English	Transliteration	Arabic
Arm	dra3	دراع
Back	Dhar	ضهر
Beard (s)	lleHya (lhee)	لحية (لحي)
Braid	dfeera	دفيرة
Bone	l3Dam	العضم
Cheek (s)	Henka (Hnaak)	الحنكة (حناك)
Chest	Sder	صدر
Ear (s)	loodn (loodneen)	لودن (لودنين)
Elbow	merfaq	مرفق
	ghrumra	الغمرة
Eye	3in	عين
Eyebrow	Hejbaan	حجبان
Eyelashes	shfaar	شفار
Face	lujah	لوجه
Finger/Toe (s)	Sba3 (SSeb3aan)	صبع (الصبعان)
Fingernail (s)	Dfr (Ddefraan)	ظفر (الظفران)
Forehead	jebha ssenTiHa	الجَبهة السَّنطيحة
Hair	sh3ar	شعر
Mess hair	sh3kaaka	شعكاكة
Hand	yedd	يدّ
Head	raas	راس
Heel	gdem	گدم
Knee	rrukba	ركبة
Leg / Foot	rjel (rejleen)	رجل (رجلين)
Lip (s)	shlaagm/ shfaayf	شلاگُم/ شفايف
Molar (s)	Darsa / Drus	ضرسة / ضروس
Moustache	moosTash	موسطاش
whiskers	shlaaRm	شلاغم

Mouth	fumm	فم
Neck	3unq	عنق
Nose	neef	نيف
	menkhaar	منخار
Rib (s)	Dl3 (Dloo3)	ضلع (ضلوع)
Shoulder	ktf	كتف
Stomach	kersh	كرش
Stomach	m3da	معدة
Teeth	snna / snaan	سنّة / سنان
Throat	Helq	حلق
Throat	Hanjura	حنجرة
Throat (animal)	qrjooTa	قرجوطة
Toe (s)	benna (bnaan)	بنَّة (بنان)
Tonsils	Hlaqm	حلاقم
Brain	mokh	مخ
Heart	qlb	قلب
Liver	kbda	كبدة
Lung	riyya	رية
Skin	jld	جلد
Tongue	lsaan	لسان
Vein	3rq	عرق

Appendix I (d) - Religious Terminology
Nouns

English	Transliteration	Arabic
Angel[16]	malak	ملك
Angel of Death (Azrael)	malak almwaat (3uzrael)	ملك الموت (عزرائيل)
Atheist	mulhid	ملحد
Buddhist	boodee	بودي
Christian	masihee	مسيحي
Church	kaneesa	الكنيسة
Diaspora	jaaleeya	جالية
Confession	3tiraaf	الاعتراف
Coptic Christian	al'aqabaT	الأقباط
Faith	eeman	إيمان
	qadar	قدار
Jew	yahood	يهود
Jews	yahoodee	يهودي
Hindu	hindee	هندي
Missionary	mubasher	مبشر
Monk	rhib	رهيب
Mosque	masjid	مسجد
Muslim	msleem	مسلم
Muslim Missionary	da3iya	داعية
Polytheist	mushrek	مشرك
Quaranic Teacher	f'qih	الفقيه
Saint	moolay	مولاي
Secret (s)	serr (asraar)	سر (أسرار)
Servant / Slave	3abd	عبد
Shrine	seyyed	سيّد
Sin	denb	الدنب

---

[16] The Angel of Death, in Arabic, has a specific name, 3zrayn/ 3uzrael from which we get 'Azrael' in English.

Soul	nefs	نفس
Superstition	Teera	الطيرة
Suspicion	shekk	شكَ
Temple	me3bed	معبد
Tomb/Shrine	qbar	قبر
	Dareeh	ضريح
Treasure	kenz	كنز

Adjectives

Acceptable	mqbool	مقبول
Envious	meHsaad	محساد
Generous	kreem	كريم
Greedy	Tmma3	طمَّاع
	qrzaaz	قراز
Humble	mutawaaDi3	متَواضع
Innocent	barie-ah	بريء
Interesting	mushawwiq	مشوَّق
	muhimm	مهمّ
Jealous	meghryar	مغيار
Miserly	sqraam	سقرام
	bkheel	بخيل
Obligatory	darooree	ضروري
	waajib	واجب
Proud	mtkbbar	متكبّر
Respectable	muHtaram	محترم
Sober	saHee	ساحي
Sufi	Soofee	صوفي
Vain	taafah	تافه

Verb	**Stem**		**First Person**	
To be holy	tqadds	تقدّس	kanqadds	كنقدّس
To believe	taaq	تاق	kanteeq	كنتيق

To betray	khaan	خان	kankhoon	كنخون
To bring Good news	bshshar	بشّر	kanbshshr	كنبشّر
To curse	sebb	سبّ	kansebb	كنسبّ
To make holy	qadds	قدّس	kanqadds	كنقدّس
To obey	Taa3	طاع	kantee3	كنطيع
To respect	Htaarm	حترم	kanHtaarm	كنحترم
To sin	d'neb	دنب	kand'neb	كندنب
to swear	Hlef	حلف	kanHlef	كنحلف
To worship	3bed	عبد	kan3bed	كنعبد

Appendix I (e) – Political Terminology

Nouns

Army/Political party	Hezb	حزب
Citizen	muwaaTen	مواطن
Civilization	HaDaara	حضارة
Coastal City	madina saheliyya	مدينة ساحلية
Coexistance	ta3aayush	التعايش
Colonization	alisti3maar	الاستعمار
Commerce	tijaara	التجارة
Competition	munaafasa	المنافسة
Criminal(s)	mujrim(een)	مجرم (ين)
Democracy	demoqraatiyya	الديموقراطيّة
Enemy (s)	3doo (3dyaan)	عدو (عديان)
Flag	raya	راية
	3alam	علم
Freedom	Hurriyya	الحريّة
Funeral	gnaza	الكنازا
Border	Hudood	الحدود
Health Insurance	taemeen SSiHHee	التأمين الصحي
Human Rights	Huqooq l'insaan	حقوق الإنسان
Immigrant	mohaajer	مهاجر
Interior City	madina dakhiliyya	مدينة داخلية
Jail	Hebs	حبس
Lawyer	mooHaamee	محامي
Minister (s)	wazeer (wuzaraae)	وزير (وزراء)
Minister w/o portfolio	wazeer bidoon Haqeeba	وزير بدون حقيبة
Opposition	mu3aaraDa	معارضة
Police	bullees	البوليس
Population	sha3b	شعب

English	Transliteration	Arabic
Production	Sinaa3a	الصناعة
Prison	Hebs	حبس
Prisoner	Hebbas	حباس
Punishment	3iqaab	عقاب
Racism	3nSureeya	عنصرية
Religious Group	jamaa3a deeneyya	جماعة دينية
Sentence (to jail)	tHkm	تحكم
Skirmishes	Hazaazaat	حزازات
Socialism	shtiraakiyya	الاشتراكي
Society	mujtama3	مجتمع
Spite	kurh	كره
Spy	jaasoos	جاسوس
Stranger	berraani	برّاني
Successor	khaleefa	خليفة
Sword	sayf	سيف
Sympathy	ta3aaTuf	تعاطف
System	Tareeqa	طريقة
Terror	khel3a	خلعة
Terrorism	irhaab	ارهاب
The Cost of Living	lmstwaaa d lma3eesha	المستود المعيشة
The Ones who Resist	muqaawemeen	مقاومين
The Resistance	lmuqaawama	المقاومة
Torture	ta3dheeb	التعذيب
Tragedy/ disaster	muSeeba kaarita maesaa	مصيبة كارثة مأساة
Treason	khiyaana	خيانة
Treaty	mu3aahada	معاهدة
Tyrant	Dhalem	ظالم

Tyrant	dictaatoor	دكتاتور
Victim	DaHiyya	ضحية
War	Harb	حرب

Adjectives

Democratic	dimoqraatee	ديموقراطي
Famous	msh'hoor	مشهور
Foreign	ajnabee	أجنبي
Homeless	msherred	المشرّد
Independent	moostaqill	مستقلّ
Political	siyasee	سياسي
Religious	Deeni-yya	دينية
Republican	jumhooree	جمهوري
Resistance	muqaawama	المقاومة
Serious, grave	m3qool/khaTeer	معقول
Sly	Hraamee	حرامي

Verb	Stem		First Person	
To vote (for)	Sawwt (3la)	صوّت على	kanSwwt (3la)	كنصوّت (على)
To elect	Ntaakhb (3la)	نتاخب (على)	kantaakhb (3la)	كنتاخب (على)
To compete (with)	Tnaafs (m3a)	تنافس (معا)	Kantnaafs (m3a)	كنتنافس (مع)
To follow	tba3	تبع	kantba3	كنتبع
To share	tshaark	شارك	kantshaarkoo	كنشاركو
To lie	kdb	كدب	kankdb	كنكدب
To illegally immigrate[17]	Hrg (l)	حرگ ل	kanhrg (l)	كنحرگ ل
To escape (from)	hrb (mn)	هرب(من)	kanhrb (mn)	كنهرب(من)

[17] Literally: "To Burn", as in burning one's identity papers.

Appendix I (f) – Naughty Words

Nouns

English	Transliteration	Arabic
Addiction	bleeya	البليّة
Adultery	zznaa	الزّنى
(also: corruption)	fsaad	الفساد
Bastard	wuld H'ram	ولد الحرام
Beer	beerra	البيرَة
Black Market	ssooq soda	السّوق السودا
Boogieman [18]	boghrTaat	بوغطاط
Booger	khnoona	خنونة
Cheater	ghrshaash	غشاش
Clatter/Ruckus	qrbala	قربلة
Complaints	shkkaawi	شكاوي
Contraband	koontraband	كونطرباند
Cute girl (lit.: small rose)	wreeda	وريدة
Drunkard	skaayree	سكايري
Glutton	wkkal	وكّال
Hashish	l'Hsheesh	الحشيش
Jerkface [19]	meeka	الميكة
Kiss	lbooss	البوس
Lie	kdba	الكدبة
White lie	kdba bayeda	الكدبة بيضة
Lies	kdoob	الكدوب
Lies	z3t	الزعت
April's fool	kdba abreel	الكدبة أبريل
Loser	khaser	خاسر
Misery/Poverty	faqr	الفقر
Nightclub	kabaaree	كباري

---

[18] Specifically, this word refers to the paralyzing monster of your nightmares, the Old Hag, the Night Terror. Or "sleep paralysis."

[19] Kind of hard to translate into English. It literally means 'plastic bag.' Shouting 'Ya meeka!' at someone is similar to 'hey, inattentive jerk!'

Noise	Sda3	ضداع
Pervert	Selgoot	صلكّوط
Pirate	qurSaan	القرصان
Piracy	qarSana	قرصانة
Problems	hamm	همّ
Pussy (i.e. weakling) [20]	micky	ميخي
Slaughter	dbeeHa	دبيحة
Slavery	3uboodiyya	العبودية
Tattoo	lushaam	الوشام
Underage Girl (literally: berry)	toota	التوتة
venereal disease (specifically syphilis)	merD noowar	مرض النّوار
Vicious	waH-shee	وحشي
Vile	qbeeH	قبيح
Violation (minor crime)	mukhaalafa	مخالفة
Weapons	slaaH	سلاح
Whores (very bad!)	q'Haab	القحاب
Witch	seHHara	سحّارة
Witness	shaahed	شاهد

Adjectives

Clever	dhkee	دكي
Clever (bad way)	khbeet	خبيت
Crazy	H'mak	حمق
Crazy (or angry)	mejnoon	مجنون
Crazy	msTTee	مسطّي
Crazy	hbeel	هبيل
Dangerous	khataar/ khteer	خطر / خطير
Dead	meeyyet	ميّت

---

[20] This refers to a certain cartoon mouse. The plural is mikyaat.

Drunk	skraan	سكران
Greedy	Tmaa3	طمّاع
Messy	merwwean	مروّن
Mischievous	basal	باسل
Nasty	qbeeH	قبيح
Naughty	Daasr	ضاسر
Nosy	fdoolee	فضولي
Sane	b3qeloo	بعقلو
Sneaky	Hraami	حرامي
Spoiled	mfeshshesh	مفشّش
Stinky	khanez	خانز
Stingy	qrzaaz	قرزاز
Stupid	mkellakh	مكلّخ
Sullen	mkendar	مكندر

Verbs	Root		First Person	
To cheat	ghrash	غش	kanghresh	كنغشّ
To constantly complain	negrez	نگرز	kannegrez	كننگرز
To give the evil eye[21]	3ayyen	عيّن	kan3ayyen	كنعيّن
To Die	maat	مات	kanmutt	كنمت
To kill	qtl	قتل	kanqtel	كنقتل
To kiss	baas	باس	kanboos	كنبوس
To poison	semem	سمم	kansemmem	كنسمّم
To smoke	kmee	كمي	kankmee	كنكمي
To spit (on)	bzaq (3la)	بزق (على)	kanbzaq	كنبزق
To steal	sraq	سرق	kansraq	كنسرق

---

[21] In a different context, this means "to appoint". Sometimes.

| To vomit | tqeeya | تقيّا | kantqeeya | كنتقيّا |
| To whore (very bad!) | znaa | زنى | kanzni | كنزني |

Expressions

Are you an idiot (donkey)?	wash nta Hmar?	واش نتا الحمر؟
Die of poison! [22]	moot bsemm	موت ب السمّ
Get lost!	ghbr!	غبر
May God kill you! [23]	Llai e3teek lmoot	الله يعطيك لموت
God's curse be on you! [24]	allah yne3lek	الله ينعلك
Go to hell! [25]	Allah 3Teek lweel	الله يعطيك لويل
Your tongue licked a dog! (i.e. God forbid!)	fmmek lhsoo kelb	فمّك لهسو الكلب

---

[22] Used to tease someone in a childish way, sort of like 'nyah nyah!'

[23] If you ever say this, and I recommend you don't, get ready to kick some ass, because whoever you said it to will be furious with you.

[24] I include this in case someone says it to you. By reading this, you agree not to say it to anyone. It's super offensive.

[25] "May God send you to Styx." In Islam, lweel is a river in hell, and the only western hell-river I can think of is the river Styx. The fact that the river Styx is the boundary to hell, and not hell proper, isn't important. It's as close as I could get. Anyway, if you say it to tease someone, you can claim you said "l'huile," the French word for "oil". They won't believe you, but they'll know you're just teasing.

Appendix I (g) – Environment / Places

Weather	Jaw	الجو
Cloud (s)	ghreeaama (leghryaam)	غيامة (غيام)
Dusty wind	l3jaaj	العجاج
Humidity	rruTooba	الرطوبة
Lightning	lbraq	البرق
Rain	shtaa	الشتا
Snow	Telj	التلج
Star	nejma	نجمة
Storm	Hamla	حملة
Storm/deluge	l'3aaSifa fayadan	عاصفة فيضان
Thunder	rr3d	الرّعد
Wind	reeh	الرّيح
Climate	TTaqss	الطقس
	mghrayyem	مغيم
Cloudy	msaHHeb	مسحّب
Cool / Cold	bared	برد
Far	b3eed	بعيد
Hot	skhoon	سخون
Near	qreeb	قريب
Stormy	mer33ed	مرعَد
Warm	dafee	دافي
Museum (s)	matHaf (mtaaHf)	متحف (متاحف)
Artifacts	tuHaf	تحف
Statue	timtaal	تمتل
Environment	bee'a	البَيئة
Desert	Sa'Hraa	صحرا

English	Transliteration	Arabic
Forest	lghraba	الغابة
Garden (s)	jarda (jraadee)	جردة (جرادي)
	lghrersa (leghraasi)	الغرسة (الغراسي)
Island	jazeera	الجزيرة
Moon	qmar	القمر
Mountain (s)	jbel (jbaal)	جبل (جبال)
Ocean	lmuHeeT	المحيط
River	nahr (classical)	نهر
River	wad	واد
Sky	ssmaa	السما
Star	nnejma	النجمة
Swamp	buHra	بحرة
Trees	shjaar	الشجر
Waves	mwaajh	مواح
Wilderness	khlaa	خلا

English	Transliteration	Arabic
Airport	maTaar	مطار
Association	jem3ia	جمعية
Bank (s)	banka (bnaak)	بنكة (بناك)
Bookstore	maktaba	مكتبة
Café	qahwa	لقهوة
Central market	sooq	السوق
Circus	circ	السيرك
	circo	السّيركو
City (s)	mdina (mdoon)	مدينة (مدون)
City Hall	baladiyya	بلدية
Country (ies)	blaad (bldaan)	بلاد (بلدان)
Delegation	mendoobyya	المندوبيّة
Doctor's Office	3iyaada	العيادة
Downtown	Laveel	لاڤيل
	lmdeena	المدينة

Festival	mehrajaan	مهرجان
Hardware Store	drogree	الدروگري
Hotel	loTeel	لوطيل
House	daar	دار
Movie Theatre	sinema	سينما
Police Station	komissariya	كوميسارية
Post Office	bosta	البوسطة
Restaurant	maT3m	مطعم
Seaport	merSa	مرصى
stable	rwa	الروا
State	wilaya	ولاية
Stock Exchange	borsa	البورصة
Swimming Pool	masbaH	مسبح
Tobacconist	ssaka	الصّاكة
Train station	lagaar	لاگار
Turkish bath	l'Hammam	الحمّام
warehouse	hri	هري
Youth Center	daar shabaab	دار الشباب

Appendix I (h) – The States

Alabama	ألاباما	Montana	مونتانا
Alaska	ألاسكا	Nebraska	نبراسكا
Arizona	أريزونا	Nevada	نيفادا
Arkansas	أركنساس	New Hampshire	نيو هامشر
California	كاليفورنيا	New Jersey	نيو جرزي
Colorado	كولورادو	New Mexico	نيو مكسكو
Connecticut	كونيتيكت	New York	نيو يورك
Delaware	دلاوير	N. Carolina	نورث كارولاينا
Florida	فلوريدا	N. Dakota	نورث داكوتا
Georgia	جورجيا	Ohio	أوهايو
Hawaii	هاواي	Oklahoma	أوكلاهوما
Idaho	أيداهو		
Illinois	ايلَينوي	Pennsylvania	بنسلفانيا
Indiana	إنديانا	Rhode Island	رود ايلاند
Iowa	أيوا	S. Carolina	ساوث كارولاينا
Kansas	كانزاس	S. Dakota	ساوث داكوتا
Kentucky	كنتاكي	Tennessee	تينيسي
Louisiana	لويزيانا	Texas	تكساس
Maine	ماين	Utah	يوتا
Maryland	ماريلاند	Vermont	فرمونت
Massachusetts	مساتشوستس	Virginia	فرجينيا
Michigan	ميشيكان	Washington	واشنطن
Minnesota	مينيسوتا	W. Virginia	وست فرجينيا
Mississippi	ميسيسبي	Wisconsin	وسكانسن
Missouri	ميزوري	Wyoming	وايومينج

Appendix I (i) – Jobs and Work

Accountant	muHaasib	محاسب
Actor	momattil	ممثّل
Ambassador	safeer	سفير
Beggar	Tllaab	طلّاب
	saa3i	ساعي
Businessman (men)	taajir (tijaar)	تاجر (تجَار)
Butcher	gzzaar	گزّار
Carpenter	nejjaar	نجّار
Clown	bahlahwan	بهلاوان
Cobbler	Terraaf	طرّاف
Conductor (train)	muraaqib	مراقب
Conqueror (good)	faateH	فاتح
Conqueror (bad)	ghraazee	غازي
Cook	Tbaakh	طباخ
Craftsman	Saani3	صانع
Dentist	denntist	دنتيست
Detective	inspektoor	أنسبكتور
Director	mudeer	مدير
Doctor	Tbeeb	طبيب
Driver	sheefour	شيفور
Driver's Assistant	greesoon	گريسون
Electrician	trisyaan	ترسيان
Engineer	muhandis	مهندس
Farmer	fellah	فلّاح
Fisherman	Sayyaad	صيّاد
Gardener	jardeenyee	جارديني
Greengrocer	khddaar	خضّار
Grocer	mool hanoot	مول لحانوت
Guardian	3ssaass	عساس
Guide	geed /giyya	گيد / گيّا
Hairdresser	kwafoor	كوافور

125

Hairdresser	Halaaq	حلّاق
Inspector	mofattish	مفتّش
Journalist	SaHafee	صحفي
Judge	qaadee	قاضي
Lawyer	mooHaamee	محامي
Lifeguard	meTr najeur	ميطر ناجور
Mason	bennay	بنّاي
Mechanic	mekanisyaan	ميكانسيان
Midwife	qaabla	قابلة
Night Watchman	biyyat	بيّات
	3assaas d lleel	عسّاس د اللّيل
Painter	rssaam	رسّام
Policeman	bulleesee	بوليسي
Professor	ustaad	أستاد
Real Estate Agent	s'msaar	سمسار
Buyer (also: spy)	beyyaa3	بياع
	zaboon	زبون
Customer	kliyyan	كليّان
Gov't employee	muwaDDaf	موظّف
Owner	mool	مول
Seller	shaaree	شاري
Administration	edar	إدارة
Company	sharika	شركة
Institute	ma3hed	معهد
Gov't profession	waDheefa	الوظيفة
Singer	mghranee	مغنّي
Soldier	3askri	عسكري
Student	Taalib	طالب
Taxi driver	mool Taksee	مول الطاكسي
Teacher	mu3allim	معلّم

126

Ticket Taker	roosoofoor	روسوفور
Tourist	saaeH	سائح
	(suyyaH)	(سيّاح)
Translator	mutarjim	مترجم
Wanderer	rHHaal	رحّال
Waiter	garsoon	گارصون
Welder	soodoor	سودور
Widow	hjjaala	هجّالة
Writer/ secretary	kaatib	كاتب
Worker	3aameel	عامل
Secretary	kaatiba	كاتبة
Shepherd	saaraH	سارح
	raa3i	راعي
Seamstress	khayaaTa	خيّاطة
Busy	mshghrool	مشغول
Hardworking	Haadeg	حادگ
	mujtahid	مجتهد
Lazy	m3gaaz	معگّاز
Not Studious	ksslaan	كسلان
	kasool	كسول
Scientific	3ilmee	علمي
Specialized	mtkhSSeS	متخصّص
Studious	mujtahid	مجتهد
Technical	tiqni	تقني

Appendix I (j) – Colors and Shopping

Beige	bij	بيج
	crema	كرمة
Black	kHal	كحل
Blue	zraq	زرق
Brown	qahwee	قهوي
Gold (adjective)	dehbi	دهبي
Gray	rmaadee	رمادي
Green	khdar	خضر
Orange	leemoonee	ليموني
	letcheeni	لتشيني
Pink	wardee	وردي
	Hmeesi	حميسي
Purple	mdaadi	مدادي
	Hmaami	حمامي
	moov	موڤ
Red	Hmar	حمر
Silver	feDDee	فضي
	nuqri	نقري
Turquoise	turkwa	تيركوا
White	byaD	بيض
Yellow	Sfar	صفر
Yellow (in Tetuan)	Hmeesi	حميسي
Light colored	meftooH	مفتوح
Dark colored	mghrlooq	غامق
Slate/stone colored	Hajree	حجري
Brass (noun)	nHas Sfar	نحاس صفر
Bronze	nHas Hmar	نحاس حمر
Copper	nHas	نحاس
Gold (noun)	d'heb	دهب
Iron	hdeed	حديد
Ivory	3aj	عاج

English	Transliteration	Arabic
Lace / thread	khayT	خيط
Lead	khfeef	خفيف
Luxury	rafaheeya	رفاهية
Fabric	toob	توب
Plastic[26]	meeka	لميكة
Silk	Hreer	حرير
Silver	feDDa nnuqra	فضّة نقرة
Steel	fuld	فولد
Timber/ wood	khsheb	خشب
tin	qezdir	قزدير
Wool	Soof	صوف
variety	shkel	شكل
Blunt	Haafee	حافي
Bright	naSe3	ناصع
Cheap	rkheeS	رخيص
Chic, stylish	mferkes	مفركس
	zaaz	زاز
Clean	nqee	نقّي
Clear	waaDeH	واضح
Comfortable	mureeh	مريح
Dirty	mwesskh	موسّخ
Expensive	ghralee	غالي
Faded / Dull	bahet	باهت
Hard	qaaSa'H	قاسح
New	jdeed	جديد
Not broken	mSwaan	مصوان
	mSlooH	مصلوح
Old (thing)	qdeem	قديم
Opaque (cloth)	ghrleeD	غامض

---

[26] Refers to plastic in general, as in 'plastic comb' but is also used for those ubiquitous shopping bags.

Round	mdewwar	مدّور
Sharp	maaDee	ماضي
Soft	rteb	رطب
Solid	qaaSaH	قاصح
	S'HeeH	صحيح
Square	mrebba3	مربع
Suitable	mnaaseb	مناسب
Worn	baalee	بالي

Appendix I (k) – Clothing

English	Transliteration	Arabic
Babushka	zeef	زيف
	fular	فولار
	sebniya	سبنية
Backpack	sacadoe	ساكاضو
Bathing Suit	mayoo	مايو
Belt	smTa	سمطة
Belt, Almoravid	hzaam mraab3lee	حزام مرابعلي
Belt, braided	mjdool	مجدول
Bib	rreeyaaga	ريالڭة
Braided cloth used to hold back a dress	Hmaala tekhmeel (northern)	حمالة تخميل
Bracelet	debliijh	دبليج
Brassiere	sutyanat	سوتيانات
Business Suit	koosteem	كوستيم
Clothes	Hwaaej	حوايج
	khrooq	خروق
	les couches (french)	لي كوش
Diaper	tsarweelaat	تسرويلات
Dress	kswaa	كسوة
Dress, Traditional	tshameer	تشامير
Earrings (small)	Twingaat	طوانڭات
Earrings (studs)	boolat	أبولات
Gloves	ligat	ليكات
Hat (s) worn under a turban[27]	shddood	شدود
Hat, Awesome	Tarboosh	طربوش

[27] The shddood as a hat to wear under a turban is an archaic phrase. Today, it refers to headware worn by women in the Rif mountains area.

131

Hat, Baseball	kaskita	كسكيطا
Hat, Snowcap	Tagiya	طاكيّة
Helmet	kask (French)	كاسك
Jacket	jakita	جاكيطة
Jeans	djeen	دجين
Leggings	leeba	ليبا
Locket	snsla	سنسلة
Necklace	3qiq	عقيق
Necktie	grvaata	كرڤاطة
Pajamas	peejama	بيجامة
Ring	khatm	خاتم
Scarf	shal	شال
Shirt, long sleeved	qameeja	قميجة
Shirt, short sleeved	qameeja nuss kmm	قميجة نص كمّ
Shirt, t-shirt	tee shoor camisita (Spanish)	تي شورت كمسيطة
Shoes	Sbbat	صبّاط
Shoes, Boots	bootyoon	بوتيون
Shoes, Flip-flops	mshshaya	مشّاية
Shoes, Sandals	Sndala	صنذلة
Shoes, Slipper(s)	bulghra bulaghree	بلغة بلاغي
Skirt	Saya falda (Spanish)	صاية فلضة
Slip (women's under-dress)	slip	سليپ
Socks	tqashr	تقاشر
Sweater / Jumper	triko	تريكو

Traditional Robe, Everyday	jellaba	جلّابة
Traditional Robe, Nice/Fancy	gandora	كندورة
Trench Coat	kboot	كبوط
Trousers	srwaal	سروال
Trousers, short	short	شورط
Underpants	slip	سليب
Undershirt	sifiteema	سيفطمة
Vest	jeelee	جيلي
Women's headwrap	hraaz	حراز

Appendix I (l) – Family (عائلة)

English	Transliteration	Arabic
Wife/Woman	mra	مرا
Wives/Women	3yaalat	عيالات
	nsaa	نسا
Man/Husband	rajel	راجل
Men/Husbands		
Girl/Daughter	bent	بنت
Girls/Daughters	bnaat	بنات
Boy/Son	wuld	ولد
	3aayl (north)	عايل
Boys/Sons	wulaad	ولاد
Parents	walideen	الوالدين
Father	ab	الاب
Mother	omm	الام
Brother	akh	الاخ
Sister	okht	الاخت
Engaged (f)	mkhTooba	مخطوبة
Engaged (m)	khaaTeb	خاطب
Fiancé(e)	khaTeeb(a)	خطيب (ة)
In-laws	nseeb(a)	نسيب(ة)
stepson	rbeeb	ربيب
stepdaughter	rbeeba	ربيبة
grandfather	jadd	جدّ
grandmother	jedda/ 3ziza	جدّة
Nephew (brother's side)	wuld khuya	ولد خويا
Nephew (sister's side)	wuld kh'tee	ولد ختي
Niece (brother's side)	bent khuya	بنت خويا
Niece (sister's side)	bent kh'tee	بنت ختي

Paternal Side

Uncle	3mm	عمّ
Aunt	3mma	عمّة
Male cousin	wuld 3mmee	ولد عمّي
Female cousin	bint 3mmee	بنت عمّي

Maternal Side

Uncle	khaal	خال
Aunt	khaala	خالة
	wuld khaalee	ولد خالي
Male cousin	wuld Hbeebi	واد حبيبي
	bent khaalee	بنت خالي
Female cousin	bent Hbeebi	بنت حبيبي
The same age	qaddqadd	قدّقدّ
Divorced	mTllq (mTllqeen)	مطلّق (ين)
Married	mzwwej(a)	مزوّج(ة)
Pregnant	Haamla	حاملة

Appendix I (m) – Animals

English	Transliteration	Arabic
Alligator	timsaah	تمساح
Ant	nnemla	نملة
	(shmmama)	(شمّاما)
Bear	ddobb	دَب
Bee	nneHla	نحلة
Black beetle	khnfoosa	خنفوسة
Butterfly	faraasha	فراشة
Cat	msh-sh	مشَ
	qeTT	قطِ
Chameleon	taata	تاتة
Chicken	djaaja	دجاجة
Cockroach [28]	sraaq zzeet	سرّاق الزّيت
Cow	bgra	بگرة
Dog	kelb	كلب
	jru	جرو
Dolphin	dilfeen	دلفين
Donkey	Hmaar	حمار
Duck	batta	بطَة
	burka	بركة
	wazza	وزّة
Elephant	feel	فيل
Fish	hoot	حوت
Flea	buq	بق
Fly	dbbaana	دبّانة
Gazelle	ghrzaal	غزال
Germ/microbe	mikroob	مكروب
Giraffe	zzarafa	زرافة
Goat	jjdee	جدي
Horse	l3awd	عود

---

[28] This literally means, ugh, "Oil Thief".

English	Transliteration	Arabic
Horse	kaydar	كيدار
Lice	gml	گَمل
	qmul	قمُل
Lion	sba3	سبع
Lizard	bobreeS	بوبريص
	zermooma	زرمومة
	wuzghra	وزغة
	teeqleet [29]	تيقليت
Monkey	qrd	قرد
Monkey [30]	z3TooT	زعطوط
Mouse	faar	فار
Parrot	babaaghra	بباغة
	pappaghrayyoo	بابغيّو
Pig	Halloof	حلوف
Pigeon	Hmaama	حمامة
Rabbit	qniyya	قنية
	qlayna	قلاينة
Scorpion	3agrb	عگرب
Sheep	howlee	حولي
Snail	baaboosh	بابوش
	ghrulaal	غلال
Snake	lf3aa	لفعى
	Hayya	حيّة
Spider	rrteela	رتيلة
Turkey	beebee	بيبي
Turtle	fekron	فكرون
Wolf	deeb	ديب
Worm	dooda	دودة

---

[29] This word is the same in Berber.

[30] Specifically, this refers to the kind of tailless monkey that organ grinders teach to perform tricks and juggle. I don't know the English word for that. This word is probably of Berber origins.

Appendix I (n) – Muscial Instruments

Personally, I can't stand music. It gets stuck in my head, and then I forget how to do math. Morocco, however, has a rich musical heritage which you may enjoy.

Banjo, 3-string	gambri	گمبري
Banjo, wide bodied 3-string	Hajooj	حجوج
Castanets	Hendka	حندكة
Castanets, obnoxious	karkba	كاركبة
Clarinet, snake charming	ghita	غيطة
Drum, bongo	taarija	تعريجة
Drum, bongo	derboogen	دربوكة
Drum, double bongo (beatnik style)	Tbla	طبلا
Drum, long bodied	goal	گول
Drum, marching	Tbal	طبال
Drummer	Tabbaal	طبّال
Drum, small	bendir	بندير
Drum, small	Tassa	طسة
Fiddle, miniature	rbab	رباب
Flute	gasba	گسبة
Flute	liyyara	ليارة
Horn, long mountain	nfir	نفير
Horn player	nefaar	نفار
Large tambourine	bouznazen	بوزنازن
Lute, miniature	suisen	سوسن
Lute, pear-shaped	l'3ood	العود
Small tambourine	Tar	طر
Tamourine, square leathern	def	دف

Appendix II – 50 Verbs

It's been said that 50 verbs account for over 90% of daily conversation. Here's my 50. Some are irregular.

Verb	Stem		First Person	
To Eat	klaa	كلى	kanakool	كناكول
To Drink	shreb	شرب	kanshreb	كنشرب
To Go	mshaa	مشى	kanmshee	كنمشي
To See	shaaf	شاف	kanshoof	كنشوف
To Visit	zaar	زار	kanzoor	كنزور
	mshaa	مشى	kanmshee	كنمشي
	3and	عند	kan3and	عند
To Travel	saafr	سافر	kansaafr	كنسافر
To Understand	fhem	فهم	kanfham	فهمت
To Want	bghraa	بغى	kanbghree	بغيت
To Learn	t3allem	تعلّم	kant3allem	كنتعلّم
To Buy	shraa	شرى	kanshree	كنشري
To Try	haawl	حاول	kanHaawl	كنحاول
To Bring	jaab	جاب	kanjeeb	كنجيب
To Run	jraa	جرى	kanjree	كنجري
To Begin	bdaa	بدى	kanbdaa	كنبدى
To Prefer	fddal	فضّل	kanfddel	كنفضّل
To Sleep	n3ass	نعس	kanen3as	كننعس
To Awaken	faaq	فاق	Kanfeeq	كنفيق
To Sit/Stay	gless	گلس	kangles	كنگلس
To Meet	tlaaqaa	تلاقى	kantlaaqaa	كنتلاقى
To Know	3raf	عرف	kan3raf	كنعرف
To Breakfast	fTar	فطر	kanfTar	كنفطر
To Lunch	tghredda	تغدّى	kantghredda	كنتغدّى
To Dinner	t3eshshaa	تعشّى	kant3ashshaa	كنتعشّى
To Study/Read	qraa	قرا	kanqraa	كنقرى

English	Transliteration	Arabic	Transliteration	Arabic
To Stop / Stand	wqaf	وقف	kanwqaaf	كنوقف
To Steal	sraq	سرق	kansraq	كنسرق
To Help	3awn	عاون	kan3awn	كنعاون
To Think	Dhann	ظنّ	kanDhunn	كنظن
To Hear/Listen	sma3	سمع	kansma3	كنسمع
To Remember	tfekkar	تفكّر	kan't'fekker	كنتفكّر
To Give	3taa	عطى	kan3tee	كنعطي
To Fight	ddaabz	دَابزّ	kandaabz	كندّابزّ
To Return/Become	rja3	رجع	kanrj3	كنرجع
To Live (right now)	skn	سكن	kanskun	كنسكن
To Live (be from)	3aash	عيش	kan3iish	كنعيش
To Write	ktb	كتب	kankteb	كنكتب
To Smoke	kmaa	كمى	kankmee	كنكمي
To Photograph	Suwwar	صوّر	kansuwwar	كنصوّر
To Rest/Lounge	rtaah	رتاح	kanrtaah	كنرتاح
To Love	habb	حبّ	kaHebb	كنحبّ
To Continue/Add/Complete	zzad kemmel	زاد كمّل	kanzeed kankemmel	كنزيد كنكمّل
To Fear	khaaf	خاف	kankhaaf	كنخاف
To Miss (someone)	twaHHash	توحّش	twaHHasht	كنتوحّش
To Rent	kraa	كرى	kankree	كنكري
To Forget	nsaa	نسى	kanensaa	كننسي
To Hope	tmenna	تمنّى	kanetmennaa	كنتمنى
To Explain	shraH	شرح	kanshrah	كنشرح
To Sing	ghrannaa	غنّى	kanghrannee	كنغنّي
To Smell (also: snort drugs)	shemm	شمّ	kanshemm	كنشمّ
To Get Drunk	sker	سكر	kansker	كنسكر

140

Appendix III – Misc. Adjectives

English	Transliteration	Arabic
Absent	ghrayeb	غايب
Active	nasheet	نشيط
Aged	shaaref	شارف
Angry	ghrDbaan	غضبان
Angry/ Sad	m3aSSeb	معصّب
Angry/Sad/Hurry	mqelleq(a)	مقلّق
Asleep	naa3s	ناعس
Average	mtwesset	متوسط
Awake	fayeq	فايق
Bad/ ugly	khaayeb	خايب
Beautiful, Pretty	zween	زوين
Big/ old/ mature	kbeer	كبير
Blind [31]	bSeer	بصير
Blind	bSra	بصرة
Blind (slur)	3eewr	عيور
Blind (slur, pl.)	3war	عوار
Broken	mahares	مهرس
Busy	mesh'ghrool	مشغول
Certain, sure	met'akked	متأكد
Close	qreeb	قريب
Closed	msdood	مسدود
Closed (used rarely)	meghrlooq	مغلوق
Cold	bared	بارد
Complicated	m3aqed	معقد
Daily	yawmiyyan	يوميّاً

---

[31] 'bSeer' literally means 'a person who sees'. (As in the English 'seer'.) To be polite, antonyms are used to describe some illnesses in Arabic as a way of telling the person you hope they get over their problem. Similarly, 'saleem' is used to describe a person suffering from tuberculosis, and literally means 'healthy person.'

Deaf	smek	صمك
Dear	3zeez	عزيز
Difficult	S3eeb	صعيب
Difficult, clever, stylish skilled	wa3er	واعر
Dizzy	daayekh	دايخ
Dry	nashef	ناشف
	yaabes	يابس
Early	bekree	بكري
Easy	saahel	ساهل
Empty	khaawee	خاوي
Enough, Sufficient	kaafee	كافي
Exhausted	mehlook	مهلوك
Famous	msh'hoor	مشهور
Far	b3eed	بعيد
Fat	ghrleeD	غليض
Fearful	khaayef	خايف
Full	3aamr	عامر
Fun	mumti3	ممتع
Generous	kreem	كريم
Good	meziaan	مزيان
Happy	ferHaan	فرحان
Harsh	Hresh	حرش
Heavy	tqeel	ثقيل
High (location, not drugs)	3aalee	عالي
Hot	skhoon	سخون
Hurried	mezroob	مزروب
Hurried	zrbaan	زربان
Impossible	moostaHeel	مستحيل
Inside	ldaaKhel	لداخل
Intelligent	dkee	دكي
Interesting, Important	muhimm	مهمَ

Known	me3roof	معروف
Large	waasa3	واسع
Late	m3aTTal	معطّل
Light	khfeef	خفيف
Little	qleel	قليل
Lost	taalef	تالف
Lost	mjlee	مجلي
Lost	mwddr	مودّر
Mixed	mkhallT	مخلّط
Modern	3aSree	عصري
Mute	zeezoon	زيزون
Natural	Tabee3ee	طبيعي
Necessary	Darooree	ضروري
Nice	Dreeyef	ضريّف
Normal	3aadee	عادي
On purpose[32]	bl3aanee	بلعاني
Open	mHlool	محلول
Open	mftooH	مفتوح
Outside	berra	داخل
Polite	m'addeb	مؤدب
Poor	meskeen	مسكين
Popular	sha3bee	شعبي
Present	Haadr	حاضر
Present	kaayen	كاين
Respectable	muHtaram	محترم
Sensitive	Hassaass	حسّاس
Short	qseer	قصير
Shy	Hash-shoomi	حشومي
Sick	mreeD	مريض
Silent	saaket	ساكت

---

[32] As in "you did that on purpose!" – درتيها بلعاني

English	Transliteration	Arabic
Skinny	rqeeq	رقيق
	D3eef	ضعيف
Small	sghreer	صغير
Small	Deyyaq	ضيّق
Spacious/Large	waase3	واسع
Special	khaass	خاصّ
Strange	ghreeb	غريب
Strong, Correct, Healthy	SHeeh	صحيح
Successful	naajaH	ناجح
Talkative	thrthaar	ثرثار
Tall/Long	Tweel	طويل
Tender (i.e. meat)	ftee	فتي
Thick	ghrleeD	غليض
Thin	rqeeq	رقيق
Thrifty	meqtaSed	مقتصد
Tight	MDeeyeq	مضيّق
	Deyyaq	ضيّق
Tired	3iyyaan	عيّان
Traditional	bldee	بْلدي
Traditional	tqleedee	تقليدي
Ugly	khaayeb	خايب
Uncomfortable	qaSeH	قاصح
Uninjured	bla jerHa	بلا جرحا
Unlikely	mooHaal	موحال
Useful	SaalaH	صالح
Warm	daafee	دافي
Weak/thin	D3eef	ضعيف
Wet	fazeg	فازگ
Wide	wasa3	واسع

Appendix IV – Conjunctions / Timing

Either / Or	imma...awlaa	إما ... أولا
In order to	bash	باش
If	waash	واش
Although / Even though	wakh-khaa	وخّا
But	walaakin	ولكن
Who / Whom / Which / That	llee	اللّي
Because	3laaHaqqaash	علاحقّاش
	Heet	حيت
Without	blaa ma	بلا ما
Wherever	feen ma	فين ما
Then	3aad	عاد
Since / When / Because	Heet	حيت
That	belli	بلّي
Especially	khoSooSan	خصوصا
That's why	3ladakkshee	علي داك الشي
Not... anything	ma... ma Htaa Haaja	ما...ما حتّا حاجة

Time Words

When	melli	ملّي
Since	men	من
Until	Hta	حتى
As soon as	ghreer/ melli	غير / ملّي
Whenever	waqt ma	وقت ما
Before	qbl ma	قبل ما
After	mnbe3d ma/melli	من بعد ما
Always	deema	ديما
Usually	ghraaliban	غالباً

Sometimes	ba3D lmarraat	بعض المرات
Sometimes	sheee merra	شي مرّة
From time To time	merra merra	مرّة مرّة
Once (in)	merra (waHda) (f)	مرّة (واحدة) (ف)
Now	daaba	دابا
Every	kull	كلّ
Never ever!	abadan	ابداً
From now on	mn daba lfooq	من دابا ل فوق
From now on	mn daba lqddam	من دابا ل قدّام
Soon	3laayn qareeban qreeb	علاين قريباً قريب
Almost/ Around/About	taqreeban	تقريباً
As long as (you)...	maHaddk maadumti	ماحدك مادمت
Between	ma been been	ما بين بين
From... to...	men ... l...	من ... ل ...
Maybe	yemken	يمكن
Rarely / Seldom	qleel feen- fayn	قليل فين- فاين
Not yet / Still	maazaal/ baaqi	مازال/ باقي
After 33	w men b3d	و من بعد
January	yanaayer	يناير
February	fbraayer	فبراير
March	maars	مارس
April	abreel	أبريل

---

33 Sometimes used as an exasperated interjection.

English	Transliteration	Arabic
May	maay	ماي
June	yoonyoo	يونيو
July	yoolyooz	يوليوز
August	ghrosht	غشت
September	shutenbir	شتنبر
October	uktoobar	أكتوبر
November	nuwanber	نونبر
December	dujanbir	دجنبر
Winter	Sh-shtaa	الشتن
Spring	rrbee3	الربيع
Summer	SSayf	الصيف
Autumn	lkhreef	الخريف
Yesterday	lbaraH	البارح
Tomorrow	ghradda	غدّا
Sunday	lHadd	الحدّ
Monday	letneen	لتنين
Tuesday	ttlaat(a)	التلات(ا)
Wednesday	lerb3a / larba3	لاربعة / لاربع
Thursday	lkhmees	الخميس
Friday	Jum3a	الجمعة
Saturday	ssebt	السبت
Minute	dqeeqa	دقيقة
Hour	saa3a	ساعة
Today	lyoom(a)	اليومة
Day	nhaar	نهار
Week	usboo3	أسبوع
	semana	سيمانة
Month	shhaar	شهر
Year	3aam	عام
Dawn	fjer	الفجر
Midnight	nuss (d) lleel	النّص د الليل

Morning	SSbaaH	الصّباح
Afternoon	le3shiyya	العشيّة
Night	lleel	الّليل

Appendix V – Misc. Idioms and Proverbs

Make yourself at home   diir kif daarek   دير كيف دارك
(lit.: Do as you do in your home)

You are stubborn   raasek qaasH!   راسك قاسح
(lit.: your head is solid)

Where have you been?   ash had lghrboor?   أش هاد الغبور؟
(lit.: what is this disappearance?)

The deal is done!   maat lklaam   مات الكلام
(lit.: the things that are being said are dead)

Don't worry!   saan ma feeh 3Dam   اللسان ما فيه عضم
(lit.: there's no bone in your mouth!)

He's not impressive   maat leeh alhoot   مات ليه الحوت
(lit.: his fish is dead.)

He has no backbone   ma3ndoosh nnefs   ماعندوش النفس

Your secret's safe with me   sirrek f bir   سرّك ف بير
(lit.: your secret is in a well)

They're all minding their own business
kull wahed dakhel sooq rassoo
كل واحد داخل سوق راسو
(lit.: Everyone waits in the market in their head)

To follow (someone) like his shadow
(also: to consider someone a role model)
tb3 shee wahed bhaal Dlloo
تبع شي واحد بحال ضلو

The opinions of the poor don't matter
lee ma3ndoo lfloos, klamoo msoos
اللي ماعندو لفلوس كلامو مسوس
(lit.: Who doesn't have money, his words are bland)

It's icing on the cake!
ghir khudra foq T3aam
غير خضرة فق طعام
(lit.: it's just vegetables on the couscous)

What doesn't kill you, fattens you up
llee maqtlaat tsmmn
اللي ماقتلات تسمن

If you want honey, you must tolerate bee stings
lee bghraa l3sl yeSbar lqris nnHl
اللي بغى العسل يصبر ل قرس النحل

Every beetle is a gazelle to his mother
kull khanfoos 3nd moo ghrzaal
كول خنفوس عند مو غزال

If you choose to be a grain, a chicken will eat you
lee daar rasoo noukhala kaynaqbooh djaj
اللي دار راسو نوخلا كينقبوع دجاج

The polite tongue can suckle the lions' breast
llsaan lm'addeb yarda3 l'beeya
اللسان مؤدب يقدر اللبية

Don't buy fish on the ocean floor
matshreesh lhoot f qa3 lbhar
ماتشريش الحوت ف قاع البحر

Appendix VI – Being Friendly

Morocco is a friendly place. This can be especially disorienting to Americans from large cities– in Philadelphia, for example, making eye contact with a stranger is strongly discouraged. This appendix covers pleasantries more widely used in cities, which do not have a religious connotation. See the next appendix for religious idioms, which are more popular in rural areas.

English	Transliteration	Arabic
Good morning	sbah lkheer	صباح الخير
How'd you sleep?	kifaash sbhtee	كيفاش صبحتي
Nice to meet you	moosharfeen	متشرّفين
How's your health?	ash habar saha?	آش خبار الصحّة
How are you?	la-baass?	لاباس؟
R: Praise God	hemdullilah	الحمد الله
R: Yo, not bad[34]	fuq figueeg	فق فـﯕﻴﮒ
Everything okay?	kulshee bekheer?	كلشي بخير؟
R: Everything's fine	bekheer	بخير
What's going on? (lit.: What's your news?)	ash habarek?	أش خبارك
How's your family?	l3a'eela bekheer?	عائلة بخير
How's your house?	daarek bekheer?	دارك بخير

(n.b.: It's more polite to inquire about a man's house than about his wife, which could lead to... *misunderstandings*.)

---

[34] Figuig is a town near Algeria. 'fuq Figuig' means 'above figuig' and is used as a joke, i.e. "Since I'm not in Figuig, things are pretty good."

| Thank you | shokraan | شكران |
| Thank you | bla jmeel | بلا جميل |

(lit.: without favor, as in, don't worry about it)

| Congratulations | mabrook | مبروك |

| Welcome | merHba | مرحبا |

| Welcome to my home | merhba bikum | مرحبا بكم |

| See you later | nshoofek min b3d | نشوفك من بعد |
| Take care of yourself | t'halla f'raasek | تهالآ فراسك |

(lit.: watch your head.)

| Boo hoo! | weelee weelee | ويلي ويلي |

(This means something like 'Oh no!' or 'boo hoo!')

| Hurry up! | deghya, deghya! | دغيا دغيا |

(lit.: fast fast!)

| LOOK OUT! | BALAK! | بالك |
| " | 3NDAAK! | عنداك |

(n.b.: This is going to be shouted at you from behind. Although it's a general warning shout for dangerous situations, most often you'll hear it from a man driving a donkey. What he means is, kindly step aside or be trampled. You may also hear "BALAK SMA3 BALAK!" which means "Look out, hear this, look out!")

Appendix VII – Religious Idioms

Everyday Phrases

Hello! [35]	ssalaamu 3alaykum	السلام عليكم
R: Hello to you!	wa 3alaykum ssalaam	و عليكم السلام
Praise be to God!	lHamdulillaah	الحمد الله
God willing	inshaa'a llaah	إن شاء الله
This is God's will	maashaa'a llaah	ماشاء الله
Trust in God	twekkel 3la allah	توكّل على الله
Let's begin! [36]	bismillaah!	بسم الله
Good night!	allah ymsseek bikheer	الله يمسّيك بخير
Goodbye! [37]	bessalama	بالسلامة
Please	allah ykhaleek	الله يخلّيك
Please	allah yjaazeek bikheer	لله يجازيك بخير
God Bless you [38]	t'baark allah 3leek	تبارك الله عليك

---

[35] "Peace be with you." The response is "and also with you." In both of
these phrases 'you' is plural because these phrases wish peace not only to
a person, but to the angel that follows that person, recording their deeds
for judgement day.

[36] "In the name of God." Used at the beginning of a meal, when getting
into a car or airplane, or (sometimes) when paying for something.

[37] "With peace." As in, "go with peace."

[38] To congratulate a friend on an accomplishment or performance, such
as releasing a Moroccan Arabic textbook. Congratulations without a
phrase like this could be construed as giving someone the evil eye.

R: God Bless you	allah ybaark fiik	الله يبارك فيك
It wasn't meant to be [39]	maktaabsh(i)	ماكتابش(ي)
With health! [40]	b'SSeHHa	ب الصحّة

God grant you health [41]
allah ye3Teek SSeHHa
الله يعطيك الصحّة

Contrary Phrases

I disagree [42]	sebHaan Allah!	سبحان الله
Shame!	Hshooma!	حشومة
Shame! (Forbidden!)	H'raam!	حرام
God Forbid!	allah yester!	الله يستر

Health Phrases

It's true! I swear! [43]	w-allah (l3aDeem)	و الله العظيم
God cure you!	allah yshaafi	الله يشافي
God preserve you	allah ynejjeek	الله ينجّيك
Gesundheit! [44]	yreHmek Allah!	يرحمك الله

---

[39] "God has not written it in the book of fate."
[40] Said to someone who has just a bath, gotten new clothes (or even a car!) or to a person who is going to have a meal or party.
[41] The response to *bSSeHHa* or *bSSeHHa w rraHa* meaning "to your health" and "to your health and relaxation," respectively. Often said to waiters or people feeding you
[42] "Glory to God!" Also used when you see something strange or wonderful, like the night sky in the Sahara or an honest faux guide.
[43] "By God!" or "By God the greatest!" Not, technically, health related.

May God guide you 45   allah yehdeek   الله يهديك

May God not show you harm   lehla ywerreek baas
(response to l'ai shaafi)   لَهلا يورّيك باس

God make your life easier   allah yesahhel
(Said to beggars)   الله يسهّل

No harm will befall you   matshoof baas
(lit.: do not see harm)   ماتشوف باس

God give you swollen lymph-nodes46   allah ye3Teek lhlaaqm
الله يعطيك الحلاقم

May God protect you (from the thing I'm suffering from)47
llehla yhewwjk
للهلا يحوّجك

May God look at your illness
allah yshoof men Haalek
الله يشوف من حالك

May you not lose your health
llehla ykhaTTeelek SeHHa
لهلا يخطيلك صحة

---

44 This is what you say to someone who says "hemdullilah" after sneezing.
45 Said to wish a person to return to good manners, stop bad habits, beat addictions, or said to an angry or misbehaving person.
46 Sometimes used to curse someone who, for instance, is talking too loudly.
47 Used by someone who was asked for a favor. For instance, you might get told this if you ask to borrow 100 dirhams from a mate. It doesn't mean he won't give it to you, it just means he is not terribly amused at the situation.

May God not make you choose between two evils
Lahla ykheyyrna f drar
الله يخيرنا ف درار

May no harm befall you
ma m'shaa maa3ak baas
مامشى معاك باس

May God help you recover
maykoon baas
مايكون باس

God forgives [48]
allah ysaamaH
الله يسامح

Formal/Polite phrases

God helps [49]	allh y3aawn	الله يعاون
God return this money [50]	allah yekhlef	الله يخلف
Goodbye! [51]	lah yhanneek	الله يهنّيك
Thank you [52]	baarak alla-hu feek	بارك الله فيك
Thank you [53]	allah yrDee 3leek	الله يرضي عليك
Thank you [54]	allah yerHam lwalideen	الله يرحم الوالدين

[48] Response to 'smeh lee' (Literally: forgive me, used as excuse me).
[49] Said to working folks with the general meaning of "have a nice shift."
[50] Said when accepting payment for something or when done eating.
[51] "God grant you a peaceful mind."
[52] "God bless you". In Fes, this is used all the time for in place of 'thank you'. In Casablanca, I was told only to use this for major issues, like donating a kidney or co-signing a lease.
[53] "God be satisfied with you." Said to young people, sons, and daughters.

Thank you	allh ykettar kheerek	الله يكتّر خيرك
Thank you/ God bless you	allah yej3al feek lbaraka	الله يجعل فيك البركة
You're welcome 55	waldeena w walidek	والدينا ووالديك
	waldeena ajamee3an	والدينا أجميعن
Sorry to mention that 56	haashaak	حاشاك
R: God make you happy	3azzek allah	عزّك الله
I agree / I hope so! (lit.: from your mouth to God)	mn fumek n'llah	من ن فمّك الله

In the name of God, the most merciful and compassionate 57
bismillah rraHmaan oo rraHeem
باسم الله الرحمن الرحيم

Travel Phrases

Bon voyage! 58
allah yweSSlek 3la kheer
الله يوصّلك على خير

Have a safe trip!
treq salaama
طريق السلامة

---

54 "May your parents rest under the blessings of God." Said even to people whose parents are still alive.
55 "Our parents and yours" or "Our parents together."
56 Said after mentioning something gross. As in "Someone took a shit in the grand piano, hashaak."
57 This is the first verse in any chapter of the holy Quran. It's said before eating, and also before doing anything involving hot water to scare away djinn, who are injured by hot water, and will haunt you.
58 "May God deliver you safely to your destination."

May God keep you safe
allah ysellemek
الله يسلّمك

Thank God for your safety
alHamdullah 3la slamtek
الحمد الله على سلامتك

Family Phrases and Condolences
God make them decent [59]

    allah ySlaH   الله يصلح

    allah ysakh-khar   الله يسخّر

    allah ysakh-khar f drarree   الله يسخّر لك ف الدراري

God find them good [60]   aajarakum allah   آجركم الله

God have mercy [61]   allah yr'Hem   الله يرحم

It's in God's power   biHawli allah   بحول الله

May God greaten the good deeds
allah y3aDDem l'ajar
الله يعظّم الأجر

May God not show you (pl) evil [62]
llehla ywerrikoom sharr
لهلا يورّيكم شرّ

---

[59] Also translated "May God raise them well." Said about children to parents.
[60] Said to comfort the bereaved after the death of a loved one.
[61] Said about the dead.
[62] Response from the family of the deceased to those who wish them well.

May God trade love for patience [63]
allah ybeddel lmHebba bSSbar
الله يبدّل المحبّة بالصّبر

May God broaden his tomb
allah yewssa3 qabroo
الله يوسع قبرو

Miscellaneous

May God increase your fortune
   allh yekttar kheerik   الله يكتّر خيرك
   allah yqawwee lkheer   الله يقوّي الخير

Happy Holidays! [64]   3waasher mbrokaa   عواشر مبروكة

R: For us and for you   3leena w 3leek   علينا و عليك

Keep secret what God has kept secret
str ma str allah
ستر ما ستر الله

What did God name you?
aash smmaak allah?
آش سمّاك الله

May God complete it well [65]
allah ykmmel bekheer
الله يكمّل بخير

---

[63] Having said this a number of times I can assure you that though a beautiful phrase, it is unlikely to make things more bearable.

[64] The holiday, in this case, is almost always Ramadan, but the phrase can be used for any festival.

[65] Said to people who are recently engaged or married.

Special Thanks

Congratulations, you made it to the end of the book! By now, you should know the appropriate thing to say is "Hemdullilah." If you know me, you know I could never have written this fancy book on my own. I had a lot of help. First: This book is dedicated to one of the finest gentlemen to be found anywhere in the world: Si Abdennebi Elhaloui.

I want to thank Saadia Maaski, Daoud Casewit and everyone at MACECE that helped run the Fulbright program in Morocco, and Michel Barsoum, Daniella Ascarelli, Dorilona Rose at Drexel University. They helped me get the grant in the first place. Also, thank you, Abderrahim Aatiq, Hassan Hannache, sweet Khadija, and Moulay Rachid Tigha at the University Hassan II in Casablanca, with whom I worked.

For reasons known to each of them, I'd like to thank Sheikh Nabil Khan, Abdullah and Lubna Dann, Elena Lloyd-Sidle, and Erica Duin; the two Megans (Mulcahey and Pavlischek), Robert and Handsome John, El Padre, Andrew Gunderson, Dustin Reynolds, and Phillipe Schol; the two Sarahs (wahed and jooj), Imelda O'Reilly, Shara and Dan van Zant, Devon Lidell, Liza Baron, Anna Gressel, and Hannah Armstrong. Marci, Elrond, Kathy, and The Wetzel also greatly contributed to my time over there.

In English, French, Latin, or Moroccan Arabic, I don't know how to express my thanks to Nicole Matuska, with whom I spent many an hour over camel tajines, and without whom my time in Casablanca would have been much less pleasant.

I'd like also to thank the people that took concrete steps to make this book a reality: George Roberson, who pulled everything together and put me in touch with his comrades at the International Centre for Performance Studies, which, under the direction of Khalid Amine, put me in contact with Rajae Khaloufi, who edited the final versions of this book. Until it got into the hands of these people, the Arabic spelling in here was horrendous. And also a special note of thanks to Simona Schneider, Dr. Jennifer A. Roberson and a number of anonymous readers and peer-reviewers who were kind enough to contribute their time, input, and expertise.

Finally, allow me to thank you, faceless reader of this book. May I suggest you read it again? As much of a pain as learning to speak Moroccan darija was, Morocco is an amazing place and it's even better if you speak the language.

Aaron Sakulich
Washington, DC

الحمد الله

Also from Collaborative Media International (CMI)

Bowles / Beats / Tangier: Paul & Jane Bowles, the Beat Generation & the crossroads city of Tangier, Morocco
Allen Hibbard & Barry Tharaud, editors
International Collaboration Series: North Africa

Shakespeare Lane: a contemporary reading of Tanjawi society - at the crossroads city of Tangier, Morocco - what will the citizens choose for their future?
By Zoubeir Ben Bouchta
A play concerning society and engagement in Tangier, Morocco; translated from Arabic to English by Rajae Khaloufi
Contemporary Voices Series: North Arica

Available worldwide on Amazon.com and other fine retailers

CMI welcomes proposals and additional collaborators. Submit manuscripts and correspondence to: collaborative.media@ymail.com

George F. Roberson, Publisher

About the cover

The cover design was contributed by Andy Reynolds, a Washington, DC-based graphic designer: andynco@earthlink.net

The front cover photo was contributed by Yiqing (CHENG, Li) of YQ studios: http://yqstudio.blogspot.com, lcheng8@gmail.com. It was taken in spring 2008 near the city center in Tangier.

The back cover photo was contributed by George F. Roberson, Fulbright Scholar to Morocco '07-'08: collaborative.media@ymail.com. It was taken in spring 2008 in the Iberia neighborhood of Tangier.